GET NOTICED.
BE REMEMBERED.

GET NOTICED.
BE REMEMBERED.

KRISTA CLIVE-SMITH

MERACK PUBLISHING

Clive-Smith, Krista, 1975-
    Get noticed, be remembered: creating a personal brand
strategy for success / Krista Clive-Smith.

Includes bibliographical
references. ISBN 978-0-9734274-2-4

    1. Business & Economics: Personal Success. 2. Self-Help. I. Title.

Published and distributed by Merack Publishing.

EDITORS
Rod Chapman
Terry Bullick

TEXT DESIGN & LAYOUT
Gail Pocock

COVER DESIGN
Jimi Scherer (Imagery)
Ashley Bunting (Content)

PRINTED AND BOUND IN THE UNITED STATES OF AMERICA

*This book is dedicated to those
seeking to answer the all important
question "Who Am I?".*

*May these teachings be the pathway
for your journey from lost to found.*

CONTENTS

ACKNOWLEDGEMENTS vii
INTRODUCTION ix

PERSONAL BRANDING 101
An Introduction to Personal Branding 3
Three Elements of a Brand Strategy 14
The Four Phases of Brand Development 24

PHASE I: DEFINING YOUR BRAND
Drawing the Blueprint: Planning and Design 29
Gathering Resources: Idea Book & Style File 32
The Importance of Values Clarification....................................36
Learning to Dream on Paper 47
The Awareness of Goal Setting 58

PHASE II: POSITIONING YOUR BRAND
Searching for Passion... and Finding It 73
Finding Your Place in the World 81

PHASE III: PACKAGING YOUR BRAND
An Introduction to Personal Style 107
Exploring Your Inner Self...114
Exploring Your Outer Self 133

PHASE IV: CHAMPIONING YOUR BRAND
You Are Hereby Guilty by Association.......................................165

CONCLUSION 185
APPENDIX..191
ABOUT THE AUTHOR...197

ACKNOWLEDGEMENTS

I truly feel like the luckiest girl on earth. The incredible blessings God has bestowed upon me are humbling to say the least, and I'm grateful every day to be living this life and to be surrounded by the amazing humans with whom I have the privilege of sharing the journey. I love you all more than words could ever say.

RYAN :: *You're the best thing that's ever happened to me.*

KENNEDY AND LINDSAY :: *Being a mom (and stepmom) is my greatest gift and highest privilege in this lifetime. I feel so honored to be able to support and guide you to becoming the best versions of your unique selves you can be.*

(MY MOM) PAT MINTERN :: *Your love, kindness, support and encouragement has made me who I am today, and our friendship is one of the greatest blessings in my life. Thank you for being the most true example of what a mother's love looks like in human form.*

(MY DAD) CLIFF MINTERN :: *I will always be your little girl, and even though you're no longer here in body the deep bond we share remains strong in spirit. With so much love and by example you taught me strength, mental fortitude, and the importance of a Postitive Mental Attitude. You introduced me to goal setting, the work of Napoleon Hill and W. Clement Stone, the fundamentals of selling, and how essential it is in life to work hard and hustle. I honor your memory as I marvel daily at the infinite footprints and gifts your legacy has left upon my life and heart.*

ASHLEY BUNTING :: *Not only did I marry the perfect person for me in my personal life, but I also found the perfect person for me in my business life with you, my amazing other half. There aren't enough words to ever convey the depth of my gratitude and love for you, or to describe the symbiotic, synergistic, read-each-others-minds and finish-each-others-sentences way that we think, collaborate and create together. You're my nonbiological sister and business-partner-meets-BFF. I'm so incredibly grateful for you, Ash.*

MY FAMILY :: *My Canadian roots and my big brother inspiration - I love you so much Kelly, Cindy, Alex, Ryley, and Kenzie Mintern — I couldn't ask for a better family. My South African Mum & Dad Ruth and Lindsay Clive-Smith — thank you for creating and raising the most kind, generous, loyal, loving, thoughtful and amazing man I have ever had the privilege of knowing, as well as my sister-in-law Fiona, Chris, Tia and Thor Knutsen-Smith. I'm truly blessed to have married into what feels like an extension of my own blood family.*

MY COACHES AND MENTORS :: *Pat McIntosh, Jennifer Packett, and Mike Benna - words don't do justice in expressing my heartfelt gratitude for your support and encouragement. You've shaped my thinking and who I am profoundly. I am where I am and who I am because of you.*

HAL GREEN :: *My soul bro and guardian angel - thank you for believing in me and for never, ever giving up. Your influence on my life - past and present - is immeasurable.*

MY SOUL TRIBE :: *Whether old or new friends, female or male, near or far — the depth of our connection and the overwhelming love I have for you is indescribable. You've supported me through my best and you've loved me through my worst. I am truly grateful for each and every one of you. Thank you for being exactly who you are.*

MY AMAZING BOOK TEAM :: *Gail Pocock, Rod Chapman, Terry Bullick, Georgina Forrest, Jimi Scherer and Ashley Bunting. For your incredible gifts and talents, and from the bottom of my heart, THANK YOU. We did it!*

INTRODUCTION

There is a wick within you that is waiting to become the light of your soul. When this inner flame burns brightly, you will feel a magnificent awakening in your life.

BRADFORD KEENEY

YOUR PERSONAL IMAGE, the one you greet the world with every day, speaks volumes about you. Your clothes, your hairstyle, even the color of your home's walls and the pictures you hang upon them may *seem* insignificant, but are in fact quite the opposite. Each contributes to, or contaminates your personal brand. Together they reflect your personality and shape others' perceptions of you.

Oprah Winfrey. Bono. Ellen DeGeneres. Madonna. Mahatma Gandhi. Taylor Swift. Princess Diana. Mother Teresa. Lady Gaga. For better or worse, these people are distinctly individual and easily recognized. They celebrate their uniqueness and understand both their strengths and their weaknesses. Highly self-aware, they've designed and cultivated a personal image that consciously magnifies their most admirable and idiosyncratic qualities. They don't attempt to hide their weaknesses, and the result is their true selves shining through, without fear of exposure. No wonder we call these people stars: they sparkle and shine with inner radiance and confidence.

Each of us is born with a talent, a calling—something that makes us unique. It's our purpose in life to fulfill that destiny, to bring to the world that which makes us great.

Finding your passion is often a matter of knowing yourself—and facing your fears. It's much like the following excerpt from the book *A Return to Love* by Marianne Williamson, as quoted by Nelson Mandela in his inaugural speech:

> "Our deepest fear is not that we are inadequate. Our deepest fear is that we are powerful beyond measure. It's our light, not our darkness, that most frightens us. We ask ourselves, 'Who am I to be brilliant, gorgeous, talented, fabulous?' Actually... who are you NOT to be? You are the child of God. Your playing small doesn't serve the world. There's nothing enlightened about shrinking so that other people won't feel insecure around you. We are all meant to shine, as children do. We were born to manifest the glory of God that is within us. It's not just some of us; it's everyone. And as we let our own light shine, we unconsciously give other people permission to do the same. As we're liberated from our fear, our presence automatically liberates others."

You might not know exactly what your destiny is, but don't be afraid. Finding it is an exciting, rewarding journey and along the way you'll find that which will complete you —the missing pieces to the puzzle of your true identity.

This book will guide you on a step-by-step tour of the different and sometimes subtle factors that define your individualism. You'll learn how to refine your own personal style while leveraging your natural talents and learned abilities into a powerful personal brand.

Years ago, when flipping through a magazine, I came across a clothing ad with a wise tagline that changed my life forever. Very simply, it read:

Be yourself. It's a very tough act to follow.

As you begin your journey down the road to the ultimate realization of what "being yourself" means to you, you'll need to assess where you are right now in this evolutionary process. Every person is at a different stage; maybe you're still trying to fit in with the masses, or perhaps you've reached the point of self-awareness that not only encourages you to be yourself, but literally demands it.

Don't worry—no matter what stage you're in, this book will help you find your true self, and much more quickly than you might imagine. Take heart in knowing that's the reason this book found you.

"But," you may be asking, "how will I know when I've arrived?"

Discovering your authentic self and creating a life you absolutely love is much like what they say about deciding on a mate: you'll just *know*. It'll feel as though at long last your mind, body, heart and soul are one, like you've come home after an extended absence. You'll feel this way because indeed you have come home: you've come home to yourself.

PERSONAL
Branding 101

An Introduction to

PERSONAL BRANDING

We are CEOs of our own companies:
Me, Inc. To be in business today, our most
important job is to be head marketer
for the brand called You.

TOM PETERS

WHAT IS BRANDING?

IN A TRADITIONAL SENSE, branding refers to ranchers searing a unique symbol (specific to their ranch) onto the hides of their cattle. The stamp is an identifier; it establishes ownership and marks the rancher's territory to the outside world.

When the rancher's cattle are shown to prospective buyers or judges, the "brand" suddenly represents more than just someone's property: it symbolizes all of the quality control standards and ranching philosophies of the owner. Over time, the ranch builds a reputation based on the level of quality and value it consistently delivers.

In more recent times, marketers have co-opted the term to describe the process of "searing" an image into the minds of consumers through the consistent use of a company's logo, slogan or tagline, marketing materials, and advertising copy.

But it's so much more than that. Branding is not strictly a function of the marketing department of a business. The brand must be infused into every fiber of the organization's being and must be championed by everyone involved, regardless of the level they work at within the company. The person answering the telephone is as responsible for the way the brand is perceived in the marketplace as the glossy ads promoting the product.

Thus, branding is truly achieved through the consistent *experience* consumers have with a company or its products or services. The definition of a brand varies from marketer to marketer, but I define it as:

BRAND

**The entire set of perceptions,
whether true or untrue, that a person holds
about an individual, company,
product or service.**

Notice I said, "whether true or untrue." Let's face it: we're human beings. While the old adage about not judging a book by its cover might sound good in theory, in reality it's rarely applied.

When you're browsing through books, how do you decide which one to buy? You may be looking for a book on branding, for example, and find several on the subject. You pick them up one by one and read the back cover.

But you don't pick up every single book in the section, do you? Chances are you only picked up the books that appealed to you when you looked at the front cover.

Personal branding is like designing the jacket for the Book of You. Authentic personal branding takes it one step further, and aligns the external reflection of who you are with your true inner essence. The goal then becomes not to design just *any* cover, but one that accurately depicts the content of the text so that readers know up front what type of book they're buying (with no bait and switch once they dive into the content).

While a brand is the entire set of perceptions a person holds, the act of branding is about proactively shaping those perceptions.

Personal branding, then, is not just the sum of the perceptions people hold about you; it's the art of influencing how others perceive you.

By creating a powerful personal and professional identity that highlights your natural talents, skills and outstanding features, you can instantly communicate your values and personality to prospective clients, employers, potential new friends or even a soul mate.

Imagine you're at a party and you're introduced to a man with hair perfectly parted down the middle and enormous, old-fashioned glasses with coke-bottle lenses. He's wearing a polyester shirt with every button done up, including the top one, and he has a pocket protector with pencils and pens neatly lined up in a row. His pants ride an inch above his waistline and the legs are too short, exposing white tube socks and gray running shoes with Velcro straps instead of laces.

What assumptions have you made about his personality, occupation and other aspects of his life based solely on his physical appearance? Plenty, I'd bet. It's human nature. You think nothing of your judgment, and you move on to the next person, hoping they'll be a more exciting prospect for an investment of your time.

After awhile you look over and "the nerd" as you've dubbed him is surrounded by a group of beautiful women on the edge of the dance floor. He takes the hand of the first in line and whisks her into a passionate tango, and then launches into a slow and beautiful waltz with the next woman waiting on the sidelines. After only two dances, he has the attention of every woman in the room, and they're all clamoring to be his next partner. He obliges each one, launching into a salsa one moment and a foxtrot the next. You're stunned. Looks can be deceiving, and you've officially been duped.

Others are doing the same thing—forming instant opinions and assumptions about *you* based on your physical appearance, whether true or untrue.

Ask yourself: is your first impression leaving people with the mental image you want them to have? Are you getting noticed for the things you want to be noticed for? Are you being remembered the way you want to be remembered? Does the image you sear into people's minds reflect your authentic self?

If you answered No or I don't know, this book is for you. Throughout the text we'll explore the subject of branding as it relates to individuals. You can utilize it as a resource guide not only to learn about personal branding, but also to help you cultivate your own authentic, memorable personal image.

WHY CREATE A PERSONAL BRAND?

Creating your own personal brand will:

- ☐ Set you apart from your competitors
- ☐ Reflect your values, personality, talent and skill set
- ☐ Increase your credibility
- ☐ Establish your expertise, authority and value
- ☐ Attract your ideal clients effortlessly

WHO IS PERSONAL BRANDING DESIGNED FOR?

A few celebrities are used in this book to illustrate key points, but it's not necessary to be famous — or even to aspire to fame — to apply the principles of personal branding with powerful results. Personal branding can help you to gain visibility in a professional context, or simply to become a living example of excellence for your children. Personal branding can be invaluable for anyone who wants to:

Lead

Inspire

Sell

Improve

Change

Teach

Counsel

Personal Branding for Parents

Parenting is one of the most difficult jobs on earth yet it remains unrecognized as a sector of the workforce when compared to "paid" professional pursuits. Most parents have never considered personal branding to be important, nor have they even heard of it as a viable parenting strategy.

By designing a powerful personal identity, you can instantly communicate your values, talents and skills to your children. You can effectively position yourself as a leader in the eyes of your offspring — not just as parents, but as important, talented individuals, separate from just being Mom or Dad. If you're like most parents, you dream of giving your children a bright future. In doing so, it's easy to lose sight of your own identity and abandon the things you once enjoyed. Time is at a premium; not only are you dealing with your own schedule, but that of your family as well.

I would encourage you to think about what your kids are subconsciously learning by the way you live your life. It's not paramount to be focused on your appearance, for example, but it is important for your children to see you making time to exercise and practicing the art of self-care. By developing your own personal brand you will be able to proactively focus on your individualism and evaluate who you are, your place in the world, how you physically appear to others, and your relationships with those around you. Chances are good if children see Mom and Dad working toward concrete goals, living a life filled with passion and pursuing activities that make them feel jazzed, those kids will aspire to do the same when they are older.

Professionals

Whether employed in a firm of 5 or 500, the name of the game in business is to get ahead. Job security is a thing of the past and increasingly, employees must stand out from the crowd if they want to advance or be promoted. You can set yourself apart by imprinting your name and abilities into the minds of your organization's key decision-makers by developing a personal brand that influences the perceptions of owners and managers, and helps attract fantastic new opportunities. Your increased visibility with your superiors will supercharge your career and put you on to the fast track to professional evolution.

People in Transition

Looking for a job? Employed, but loathe what you do? Need a change, but don't know where to start? Creating a personal brand begins with an intensive personal and professional development and self-discovery program designed to help you find your authentic inner persona and your life's passion. Once you determine who you are, you can then determine where you best fit in the marketplace in terms of job positioning.

Many clients who have completed my personal branding program have discovered their life's work and/or found their passion. Some have gone on to change careers, while others have taken the next step and started their own businesses. Others have found their dream job and are now energized by the thought of going to work each day, instead of feeling uninspired and even dreading getting out of bed each morning like they did before.

Youth

If only I'd tapped into the idea of creating a personal brand strategy when I was younger, I'd have been so much happier during those painful teenage years when I struggled to find myself. It was in my mid-twenties that

I figured out much of my authentic identity, and even then, it was a trial-and-error process filled with lots of mistakes and mishaps. I feel fortunate that I was able to achieve this level of self-awareness reasonably early in life; for many people, it's much later in their personal evolution when they start to feel as though they have finally "arrived." By providing teenagers with the tools to develop their own personal brands, we are encouraging them early on to fully accept themselves, celebrate their uniqueness and avoid attempting to be someone they're not.

With so many career and personal choices available to kids today, it's no wonder many kids have no idea what they want to do with their lives after graduation, or what they want to be when they grow up. Peer pressure is at an all-time high, and bullying in our schools has become common. For young people to become the strong leaders who will guide us into the future, we must help them grow into confident adults with healthy self-images, an abundance of self-esteem and a secure belief in their own abilities.

Personal branding helps youth on the brink of adulthood look at their likes and dislikes and discover their innate strengths and weaknesses. It can also help them design a life plan that showcases their unique talents to the outside world, including prospective employers, new friends and even future mates.

Entrepreneurs and Small Business Owners

If you own a small business or are starting a company, personal branding is not just an option for success: it's criteria. Based on consumer habits, we know that corporate branding is an effective method of shaping public perceptions about a product or service, and thus it makes sense that entrepreneurs must do the same. The beauty of being a sole proprietor is that you have the luxury of only answering to one boss: you. This allows you the freedom to shape the business philosophy and corporate image to mirror your own personal preferences so that all aspects of your company reflect your authentic self. By doing this, you will automatically attract like-minded customers who share and admire similar ideals. As well, you will find yourself doing business with clients and suppliers who you genuinely like and trust, and your work will be more fun and profitable.

Executives and Managers

John Seely Brown, formerly of Xerox, hit the nail on the head when he said, "The job of leadership today is not just to make money, it's to make meaning." That goes for every facet of management, starting with the CEO or business owner and running through all levels of the organization. It's about touching the lives of the people around you and impacting both the company's internal and external customers in a positive way.

Personal branding provides a springboard for the cultivation of a unique and powerful style of leadership. By showcasing the humanity of those at the highest level of the organizational chart, it also affords employees in all ranks the freedom to admit to mistakes and not feel it necessary to cover up failures. It turns the management team into a group of positive role models for employees and a magnet of inspiration that makes customers genuinely want to be part of the company and the buying experience.

Sales Professionals

Research shows that people buy based on emotion more than logic. You need to know how to tap into those emotions—in a moving and meaningful way—if you're selling a product or service. Personal branding provides an emotional hook that gets customers interested in the sales process by attaching a human face and name to a product or service. By showcasing your strengths as well as your weaknesses you provide consumers with someone "real" that they can identify with and trust. That openness and clear communication style gives you a strategic advantage over your competitors because people want to deal with straight-shooters that are up front and honest with them.

Corporations

The power of personal branding is evident not only in the individual success stories of many human beings, but it is also a viable endeavor for companies that want to give their corporate brand greater impact. Here's a list of large companies in a variety of industries that have utilized personal branding by developing characters and personalities who add a human element to an otherwise impersonal brand, product or service (even if fictional or an animal):

Orville Redenbacher	*popcorn*
The Glad Man	*garbage bags*
Green Giant	*packaged vegetables*
Aunt Jemima	*syrup*
Ronald McDonald	*hamburgers*
Michelin Man	*tires*
Pillsbury Dough Boy	*pre-made baked goods*

Statue of Liberty	*New York City*
Mr. Clean	*all-purpose cleaner*
Colonel Saunders	*fried chicken*
Mickey Mouse	*amusement park*
Geico Gecko	*insurance*

With the exception of Mickey Mouse and the City of New York, each of the above characters initially represented some pretty standard product offerings. While it may have been tough sledding early on, the fact that these companies went on to be leaders in their categories is a testament to the power of personal branding.

Human moments and personal connections work. Regardless of whether you're flogging garbage bags or radial tires, if you give people a face to attach to your company, product or service, they remember it. In a world filled with impersonal brands in the mass market, those with tangible human element win.

Finally, personal branding can be an effective proposition for large companies in helping their employees to better align with the corporate brand. Each company has its own unique corporate culture that exists to inform employees in a lead-by-example training method what is expected of them. The corporate culture of an organization dictates how employees dress, conduct themselves, and behave ethically at work. Strong or weak, it emerges through the consistent repetition of a particular set of images — namely those attributes the company's ideal employee would possess. By proactively cultivating a personal brand image that reflects the company's value set and personality, other employees have a realistic ideal to strive toward, inspiring them to buy in to the image and "live" the company's brand.

Three Elements of a

BRAND STRATEGY

*It's clear today's celebrities are becoming Brands.
But now even middle managers can get into the act.
So if you see your VP of Finance in the gossip
pages next to J. Lo, don't be surprised.*

FORTUNE MAGAZINE

THREE MAJOR ELEMENTS ENSURE SUCCESS in the creation of your personal brand strategy. These three elements are:

CLARITY

CONSISTENCY

AUTHENTICITY

These elements are non-negotiable. They're the law. You can't pick and choose from the list; all three elements must be present. Sure, you can get by with two out of the three if you're a flash-in-the-pan operator, but not if you want to be successful over the long term. It's all or nothing.

THE FIRST ELEMENT: CLARITY

Being clear about who you are and what you stand for is the cornerstone of your personal brand. It's the foundation upon which everything else, including your signature style and personal image, is built. Clarity will help you get noticed among your competitors, and you need clarity to effectively communicate your brand promise. (A brand promise answers the question: "What's in it for me?")

You might think that developing a safe image with universal appeal is the way to build a strong personal brand. In reality, the opposite is true. Your brand must be specific and focused on what you have to offer. As we discussed earlier, if you keep the analogy that you're developing the cover for the Book of You in mind as you go through the process, you may find it easier to remain on track. By the time your book goes to print you need to know what type of book it is, what it's about, the title, what section of the bookstore best fits the content, what the cover design looks like, the target audience you're trying to reach, and the retail selling price. In order to provide answers to each point you must have clarity—the first element in any successful personal brand.

To see exceptional personal branding in action, look no further than your closest TV. Dramas, sitcoms, reality shows, and celebrity real-life sagas fill up our down time, inviting us to tune in to see what happens this week to the characters we've come to know so well. There's a lot to be said for this trend if you consider its success in a marketing context. With reality TV and the lives of our favorite stars, the viewer involvement comes in the form of detailed character development. A show like Seinfeld, for example, is a self-proclaimed "show about nothing." But as its ratings proved year after year, it was far from that. Over time, we as the audience began to feel as though we personally knew the characters. There was a consistency in the characters' actions and speech patterns, and often we were so familiar with each one that we knew exactly how he or she would react in a particular situation. Knowing this, we still waited with anticipation to watch it unfold and laughed every bit as hard, or perhaps even harder, because of that fact.

The same idea is prevalent in many other successful shows, from children's programs to late night talk shows. Although they are diverse in subject and audience, the common thread is undeniable: each one has utilized personal branding and character development to emotionally 'hook' the viewer. Shows like American Idol, Survivor, Friends, America's Got Talent, and Oprah are just a few — the list of examples could go on and on.

If you were to take a look through history, the same trend applies. We as human beings like to, and have always liked to, be a part of things we know because it makes us feel like we're part of an "inner circle." Think back to the theme song for the old hit series Cheers... "Where Everybody Knows Your Name." Even if the characters on TV don't talk directly to us, we know them so well in our own subconscious minds it's as though we've developed a relationship with them somehow. Transcending genres without diluting its effectiveness, this is the power of personal branding.

Once you've determined who you are and what you're all about, the law of clarity must continue to be front and center in the way you communicate your specialty and expectations to the world.

I do a lot of driving, and many times I find my own clarity behind the wheel on long stretches of highway. That's my prime thinking time — on the road between speaking engagements and client meetings. On one of my trips through Western Canada I noticed that the highway signs for passing lanes differed by province. Although the signs communicated the same message, the wording was slightly different. Just by changing a few words, it dramatically altered the effect of the sign. Take a look at the difference:

```
┌─────────────┐   ┌─────────────┐
│  SLOWER     │   │   KEEP      │
│  TRAFFIC    │   │   RIGHT     │
│  KEEP       │   │   EXCEPT    │
│  RIGHT      │   │   TO PASS   │
└─────────────┘   └─────────────┘
```

Whether you consider yourself "slower traffic" or not, the clarity of the sign on the right leaves nothing open to interpretation and clearly communicates what's expected of the driver.

Just as it's important to be clear about what you want, who you are and what you can provide, you must also be clear about what you *don't* want, who you *aren't*, and what you *won't* stand for. When you're able to successfully communicate these things, your target market will define itself. By authentically being yourself and telling the universe what you want, you'll begin to attract your ideal customers: people who want what you deliver.

THE SECOND ELEMENT: CONSISTENCY

When I began to realize that I, like most people, am a creature of habit, it struck me as rather unpleasant. Somewhere along the way the idea was planted in my head that to be a creature of habit equates to being boring, and I don't think anyone wants to be boring, least of all me, a self-proclaimed fun maker and thrill seeker!

*We first make our habits, and
then our habits make us.*

JOHN DRYDEN

Along with my realization that most of us are indeed beasts following ingrained patterns came another epiphany: maybe that's not such a bad thing. In fact, I've begun to believe it's more than okay — it might even be necessary for our long-term success. As Aristotle said, "Excellence is an art won by training and habituation. We do not act rightly because we have virtue or excellence, but rather we have those because we have acted rightly. We are what we repeatedly do. Excellence, then, is not an act but a habit."

When you're clear about your brand image, the disciplined repetition of key messages about that image will help you be remembered in the marketplace. The principle of consistency helps train those around you into a belief system about your values and personality, while creating an expectation about what you can do and how you will perform. It takes time and repetition to build a habit, and the same is true for building a powerful personal brand.

When you repeat the same fundamentals over and over again, your target audience will begin to assume that you provide consistent results. This will promote trust in your performance, which will in turn help you gain loyalty among your followers. Conversely, if you're not continuously projecting the same brand image, you're sending mixed messages to the people around you. These mixed messages can destroy your credibility, confuse the heck out of your audience, and make it extremely difficult to associate any amount of power with your name and image.

> *Habits are like a cable. We weave a strand*
> *every day and soon it cannot be broken.*
>
> HORACE

The best way to communicate the concept of consistency is to have you imagine that you are planning to franchise yourself as a human being. To do this, you'll need to develop a standardized methodology for your personal presentation style. This will include determining a personal uniform, a marketing style for your distinctive talents, qualities and skills, and a code of ethics for your new company — the Company called You.

In the corporate arena, franchising continues to be one of the most successful forms of business operations. This isn't surprising, really — consumers know up front what to expect and what they'll get when they walk into a franchised business, thanks to consistency of the brand experience.

John Naisbitt Thompson, author of the book *Megatrends*, writes, "Franchising is the way of the future. Almost any service imaginable will be franchised, and many independent businesses will be absorbed by franchising. Franchising is the most successful marketing concept ever created."

In a study by the University of Toronto on the performance of franchised businesses, the data makes a compelling case in favor of this method of operations.

"...in six of the seven categories the franchised companies' performances ranged between 34 per cent and 314 per cent better than owner-managed businesses in terms of gross sales." The report credited the companies' greater success rates (in terms of gross sales) to:

Brand-name recognition

Superior marketing

Superior training

Superior buying power

In addition, the study found that 40 per cent of all non-franchised businesses don't survive the first five years of business, and of the 60 per cent that do survive, 90 per cent will fail within the next five years. At the end of the same five-year period, over 90 per cent of franchised businesses will still be operating.

By applying the franchise principle to your personal brand, you can instantly communicate what people can expect and what they'll get when they deal with you. With time and consistent self-expression, you'll develop a loyalty amongst your followers that will not be broken, even if you stumble occasionally. The key to this, however, is the final link in your personal brand strategy: authenticity.

THE THIRD ELEMENT: AUTHENTICITY

It's entirely possible for a brand to be successful—for a while—with only the first two elements, but for long-term impact the third element, authenticity, must be present. This means staying true to who you are in your most focused core. It means not attempting to be everything to everyone. It means abiding by the guiding principles you've chosen to follow and living those principles daily — setting an example through each and every action, whether someone is watching or not.

Let's use Martha Stewart and Oprah as examples. Clearly, they're two powerful female brands. One dead giveaway is that their first names can be used as a standalone without too many people wondering, "Martha who?" or, "Who's Oprah?"

Although both women are well-branded from a marketing standpoint, dramatic differences exist in the underlying foundation of each woman's brand promise.

Martha's brand was — until her legal woes — based on making even the smallest detail of domestic life remarkable. Her magazines are filled with fabulous decorating, organizing, gardening, entertaining, cleaning and holiday tips. She's set new standards for home décor and gracious living. And the best part is how easy she makes it all look, from her hospital-corner bed-making technique to the paper frills on the drumsticks of her perfectly golden Thanksgiving turkey.

Martha's brand is clear and consistent — no question about that. But there is a breakdown in the authenticity element. When you realize her brand is based on perfection, red flags should go up. Martha Stewart, like the rest of us, is a human being, and the nature of being human is that no one is perfect. It's pretty tough to uphold the brand promise of perfection for a lifetime, especially when living in the intense glare of the media spotlight. As we all know, she was eventually "found out" when the insider trading scandal broke.

If we're outraged when there's a crack in the façade, it's because we've realized there is a façade and we're not dealing with the real thing. We view her and her company as being one and the same, with no separation between her corporate brand and her personal brand. We assume she stands for the same things and abides by the same values and principles both as a human being and as a CEO. When there's a gap in the integrity between her words and actions, we feel ripped off as consumers and betrayed as friends (even though in reality we haven't ever been friends — we don't even know each other). When we learn that brand integrity is non-existent, we may eventually forgive, but we will undoubtedly never forget that breach of trust.

Now, let's look at Oprah Winfrey and her personal brand as it relates to authenticity. Right from day one Oprah has incorporated humanity into her brand: she laughs and cries with her audience and she has been on every diet imaginable, sharing with us the heartache of obesity, the thrill of weight loss and the constant struggle to keep it off. She has never maintained an image of perfection. Her brand promise is firmly rooted in the sharing of all facets of the human experience, whether uplifting, tragic or heartwarming—not just the good. She, too, has been tested. In early 1998 in Amarillo, Texas, Oprah faced civil charges of fraud, slander, defamation and negligence in a $100-million lawsuit in the much-publicized "Beef Trial" over comments made about beef safety on her TV show in April 1996.

Even while under attack in Texas, Oprah knew millions of viewers were depending on her. She honored her commitment to her fans by moving her show to Amarillo, spending nine hours each day in the courtroom and taping two shows back to back each night. She rewarded her fiercely loyal supporters around the globe by not giving in when times were tough and by remaining strong, consistent with the brand image she has developed. In the end, her brand did not suffer under the strain of the accusations and the negative press—in fact, for many of her followers the bond became even stronger.

Authentic branding is important for another reason besides the forgiveness factor when you slip up (as you inevitably will). By choosing to consciously cultivate a brand image that reflects the authentic strengths and perceived shortcomings of your personality, you attract like-minded people to you. Authenticity is about being upfront and honest: no false advertising. When there isn't a good fit, others will know right away they're better suited for a different service provider, friend or mate.

One of my clients was a "purple person". Not many colors can be associated with a specific personality type, but I think purple does happen to be one of them. You can see purple people coming a mile away. Some of my most unique and distinctly individual friends are purple people: well put-together and particular, they know exactly what they like and what they don't like. When I went through my purple client's marketing materials, she had removed most of her true personality and was using a color scheme and company name that was decidedly more corporate and, well, boring. She's a larger-than-life type of person, and yet to look at her identity package you would have thought she was conservative and passive. The clients she was attracting couldn't handle her assertive style, and she felt as though she was constantly struggling with them, diluting her suggestions so as not to offend them. When she changed the look, feel and tone of her materials to match her robust personality and colorful presence, she removed the gap between her authentic inner self and the external manifestations of that self. Her new packaging utilizes language similar to the direct way that she speaks, and she's replaced the muted pastel elements with bold splashes of black, white and — you guessed it — purple! She is now attracting vibrant and dynamic clients, many of whom are also purple people, who accept and welcome her no-nonsense approach.

The Four Phases of

BRAND DEVELOPMENT

Your level of success in life
is directly proportional
to your level of
planning and control.

CHARLES GIVENS

BUILDING YOUR PERSONAL BRAND is similar to building a house. Its phases of development follow a definite order, ensuring that once built, it will remain standing even despite fierce weather conditions.

The four phases of the development of your personal brand are as follows:

PHASE I: Defining Your Brand

PHASE II: Positioning Your Brand

PHASE II: Packaging Your Brand

PHASE IV: Championing Your Brand

Continuing with the analogy of building a house, the corresponding four phases in the designing and building of your new residence are:

PHASE I: Laying the foundation

PHASE II: Choosing the lot and your
             new neighborhood

PHASE III: Building your home: furnishing,
             decorating and landscaping

PHASE IV: Choosing who to invite into the inner
             sanctum known as your home

Different people will have different opinions and levels of interest in your new home. It's the same with your personal brand. You and your family will care very much how structurally sound the house is. Your friends, however, will probably focus on how it looks in terms of the design, décor, furnishings and landscaping. This is similar to your brand image: you and your family care more that you are happy, healthy and structurally sound as a human being, while others notice — and judge you based on your physical appearance and personality.

The beautiful thing about the four-phase system of brand development is that it starts with a solid blueprint, then pours a strong foundation, takes shape with the added flair of packaging, and maintains the image with the support of a strong network. This concrete, step-by-step plan ensures nothing is missed.

With this basic understanding of the task at hand, let's get started. It's time to start shopping for floor plans!

DEFINING
Your Brand

Laying the Foundation

Drawing the Blueprint

PLANNING AND DESIGN

*If I had eight hours to
chop down a tree, I'd spend six
sharpening my axe.*

ABRAHAM LINCOLN

As DISCUSSED IN THE PREVIOUS SECTION, building your personal brand strategy can be compared to the process of building a house. This same process can also help you start a business, go on a vacation or get married.

So where should you begin when the scope is so huge? You need to start with a plan.

Planning forms the framework for your life; it gives you, as the French say, a raison d'être, or a reason for being. The term "goal setting" is really just a fancy way of saying that you've mapped out some definite plans for the future. What you decide to call your plan is irrelevant — the most important thing is that you make sure to take the time to actually sit down and do it regularly, *in writing*.

Imagine living as a ship sailing out on the sea of life. Without goals or a plan, you'll drift randomly, not knowing where you'll end up or when you'll get there. You'll wake up every day wondering in which direction the winds will blow you.

"But that's great!" you exclaim. "Just imagine all the wonderfully different things I'll see! Every day will be like Christmas morning, filled with anticipation and excitement!"

Perhaps. But what happens when the wind blows your ship into a deserted bay, or when there's no wind for weeks? What happens when you realize you didn't bring enough food, and you haven't seen land in days? Or the fateful moment when Mother Nature blows you into a giant storm? Worse yet - what happens when you awake to a thunderous bang and discover the wind has crashed your ship into a reef? Without a charted course, each of these scenarios is entirely plausible.

Even *with* a charted course, you may run in to any of these situations, but if you have a plan chances are good you'll handle them differently. With a plan, the general landscape will be more familiar, even if you haven't physically been there before, because you'll have been there thousands of times in your mind. You'll have a map showing the bays, harbors and reefs. You'll be able to choose where you want to explore and where you want to avoid. Your ship will have an anchor, and you can stop to enjoy the places you find along the way. You'll have budgeted the time and distance between ports where you can buy food, so you know you'll never go hungry. You'll be able to read the skies and steer your ship away from the path of a storm. Even if you end up in foul weather, you'll be prepared with the right gear and the right navigational tools and skills.

The result? You'll end your journey with an enormous sense of satisfaction and fulfillment, because your trip was customized and specifically tailored to the desires of your highest self. You'll have been at the helm with full control over your direction, steering the ship to all the places you wanted to see and skipping the others. There will have been times when you pulled into a harbor and didn't much like it, but even when things didn't go according to plan you would've been able to get back on the ship, turn it around and leave.

Before you can even begin to formulate a plan or set goals, however, you must first close your eyes, sit back, relax, and let your imagination run wild.

Gathering Resources

IDEA BOOK
& STYLE FILE

*To know what you prefer instead
of humbly saying 'amen' to what
the world tells you is to
keep your soul alive.*

ROBERT LOUIS STEVENSON

I HAVE A RED NOTEBOOK I often cart around, which I call my Idea Book. Within its pages I write down quotes that resonate with me, ideas for businesses to start, inventions the world can't live without, titles of must-read books, great CDs or movies, and answers I come up with to questions that have been plaguing me. I include clippings of hair-styles, cars and clothing I like. My Christmas and birthday wish lists are there, along with my annual list of goals and action steps for my current six month focus. The top of every new entry is dated, with the exception of the pages of lists. Those are generally on undated pages so that I can simply flip back to that heading and continue the list as I think of new things to add. It's vitally important to the development of your personal brand that you, too, utilize such a notebook. It will allow you to chart your progress as you uncover your authentic self.

I would encourage you to go out and buy a brand new notebook (unless you happen to have one at home that you absolutely love and have been saving for a special purpose). Make sure it's portable enough that you can carry it around for whenever inspiration may strike. Choose one that speaks to you through its color, texture and/or cover. Ruled or plain pages, it's up to you — the most important feature is that on some level it really appeals to you. The reason is simple: you want it to be your first firm stand on who you truly are and who you're becoming. Consider putting any or all of the following in your Idea Book:

Quotes

Books to read

Photos of things that you like

Goals

Ideas & thoughts

Personal development exercises & answers

Questions to ponder

Anything and everything related to you!

As we progress through the four phases of personal brand development, you'll complete a number of exercises relating to your preferences, and the things that uplift and inspire you. Throughout the text are spaces to jot your answers in rough draft. I would then encourage you to rewrite your answers in your Idea Book, giving you a good dose of motivation and getting you into the habit of utilizing this resource regularly.

For those of you who prefer to keep everything electronically, I would urge you to still keep a paper-based Idea Book. You can utilize Evernote or another electronic system for brainstorming, but I would invite you to go the extra mile to create even just a highlight reel that is in notebook form on paper. Over time my collection of past (full) Idea Books have truly become some of my most valued possessions, and they are one of the first things I'd grab if I had to evacuate my home in an emergency. This collection of notebooks show the evolution of my thoughts, and tell the story of who I've become with each passing year. Electronic records can do the same, but as technology changes there's an ever decreasing chance that future generations will be able to pass this information down & open/access the electronic files. Just as floppy disks were at one time cutting edge, it's unlikely now you would have the hardware (or frankly the motivation) to find and open files from your grandfather or grandmother on one, versus flipping through a paper notebook filled with pictures and handwritten notations of their hopes and dreams.

The second item in your personal brand development toolbox is what I like to call the Style File—a manila folder with bold lettering across the tab. Anytime you're flipping through a magazine or find a photo of something that appeals to you, whether it be an outfit, a hairstyle or the way a living room is decorated, tear it out and put it into the folder. Even if you don't know why you like a particular photo, put it in the folder.

This is the one area in which I believe going digital definitely makes sense versus retaining it in paper form exclusively (I have one single paper Style File folder, but utilize Pinterest for everything else).

I love interior design, so I've created a pin board called For The Home, as well as ones for fashion, holidays, hairstyles, etc. Whenever I've moved into a new house or have the urge to revitalize a room, I look through my pin boards and glean ideas on what changes I'd like to make from the pictures I've pinned from hundreds of ideas both on Pinterest and from the web at large. Simple and easy, and as a bonus I can mix and match from many of the elements throughout the boards to get the desired look I'm after.

Your Idea Book and Style File will showcase your own preferences and the things you love. Over time, you'll begin to see patterns that you, too, can incorporate into your personal brand.

For example, in one personal branding session I flipped through my client's Style File and the dominant packaging element of her brand was immediately clear. She'd pulled out page upon page from magazines of models wearing suit jackets, and although they all looked different because they were in a variety of colors and patterns, upon closer inspection we noticed the jackets were all the same cut. The style happened to work for her body type, and she already owned a few jackets that looked similar to the ones in the pictures, so that became her basic signature element - and the beginning of her personal brand "uniform."

After you get a feel for your preferences in terms of external appearances, the next step is to turn the focus inward. This step will assist you in determining what you, as a distinct individual in this world, like and dislike.

The Importance of

VALUES
CLARIFICATION

*It's not hard to make decisions
when you know what your values are.*

ROY DISNEY

V ALUES ARE DEFINED AS "the established ideals of life."
They're the things we hold near and dear to us. Comprising
the filters and perceptions through which we see the world,
they're the core qualities we stand for. When things aren't
working for us, our values are an excellent place to begin
the detective work of finding out what's wrong. Often we
find the struggle is either due to undefined values, or a
conflict between our goals and our stated value system.

As you start defining your personal blueprint and begin
structuring your preferences and tastes, the most important
step in your personal brand development begins with
laying the foundation: determining your values. Your
personal image is an important role because it's the basis
for the initial impressions and judgments people make
about you, but your value system makes up the core of
your personality. It speaks most strongly about who you

are as an authentic individual. Your values also form the basis for your internal integrity meter — the benchmark and rating system that at the end of the day reveals how you measure success.

When figuring out your personal value system, the most important thing is to be brutally honest with yourself. When I did this exercise for the first time I was much younger and I found it much easier back then to be honest with myself. Each January, instead of setting out a list of New Year's Resolutions, I do a goals retreat session where I sit down with my current and my past Idea Books. At the top of each page I write out headings for each of the exercises in this book. One by one, I redo the exercises to gauge where I am in my life, and where I want to be next year at this time. It's eye opening to look back over the years and see how my answers have differed — to see how my ideal day has changed, and to see how honest I have (or haven't been) with myself.

The key to loving how you live is knowing what it is you truly love. Think of one thing that would give you a genuine moment of pleasure today, and do it.

SARAH BAN BREATHNACHT

The values list reveals your personal truth, and I've often used it to analyze my life and what was happening during the times when I wasn't being my authentic self. My values were different, and they reflected what was going on in my life at the time: when I was in college, when I was working, when I got married, when I was hanging out with a particular group of friends, and when I was being seriously committed to forging my own path and not being afraid to be who I truly am. Lists compiled in the latter mindset, the "honest" lists, have remained constant throughout my life. The first time I did the values exercise, my top ten values looked like this:

Top 10 Values   DATE: Aug. 11

   1. A close relationship with parents & family

   2. Good health

   3. Travel to exciting places

   4. Friendships

   5. Wealth

   6. Controlling my own business

   7. Meeting the "right" person

   8. Respect from others

   9. Knowing accomplished & successful people

  10. Power/Fame

Conclusions that can be drawn from this list: One, I wasn't married or even in a serious relationship at the time. Two, I was unafraid to list — or value — things such as wealth, knowing accomplished and successful people, and power/fame. As the years passed, I started to see other things appearing on my top ten list like contributing time, knowledge, or money to others; peace of mind; a meaningful job or career — things I thought I *should* have on my list or that might make me more of a 'complete' person.

For many years I volunteered and employed philanthropic pursuits merely because I felt so blessed to have such a wonderful life that I felt like I should give back in exchange. I failed to realize that how I went about giving back actually mattered, and making meaningful connections to people and worthwhile organizations that I really believed in was more important than what volunteer position would look best on my CV. I was on the executive for dozens of causes, and although to an outsider it appeared as though I was a model citizen, on the inside I sure didn't feel it. Not once did I look forward to any of the meetings; in fact, I almost dreaded some of them! I would put on a brave face, smiling and participating, but would arrive home with an empty feeling I knew just wasn't right.

Finally, I decided to take six months off from every committee, board and charity. I used that time to figure out what I wanted to do with my life, and to determine what was important to me. Instead of participating in external causes, I focused on small, seemingly insignificant, internal causes that made me feel really good inside — random acts of kindness. I told and showed the people who made a difference in my life the impact they had on me. I began giving away my love, instead of just my time.

The simplest things were sometimes the best, like giving homemade jars of antipasto I'd made to my mailman and elderly neighbors at Christmas. The look of surprise and joy on their faces made me happier than in all my years of random board positions because it was direct impact, and it *felt good*.

The purpose of values in our life is to make meaning. They are our heart notes, the underlying messages behind everything we do. I once heard a quote, "What a person says he wants is of little importance, but why he wants it is of profound importance." Your values are that "why." When your values aren't clearly defined or are in conflict with your goals, you often feel paralyzed or broken inside. Once you find the personal values that speak to your highest self, you'll realize a new energy in your life, an awakening of sorts. You'll finally understand part of your life's mission, and be motivated in a greater sense than ever before to wake up each morning and live your best life.

I, too, was motivated to a greater sense after the six-month hiatus from volunteer and community work when I found out about Junior Chamber International (www.jci.cc) — a federation of young leaders and entrepreneurs, all under the age of forty.

I attended my first meeting, and I'd never in my life been surrounded by so many positive, upbeat, friendly, spirited, ambitious, high achievers all in one room until that moment. It was mind-boggling. I attended a national convention, and an area conference, then a world congress. Every person I met through these events was a vastly different individual, and worked in a completely different field, but an undeniable common thread connected them to the others in the group. It took me a while to pinpoint just what it was, but I soon discovered it: their attitude. Many of the members JCI represents in the more than 120 countries around the globe are entrepreneurs; even those who aren't still have large doses of the entrepreneurial spirit running through their veins.

In my previous philanthropic pursuits I had assumed enjoyment wasn't necessarily part of the deal. I had contributed in many ways but was always left unfulfilled. Now when I do any type of volunteer work or join a committee, the work has been carefully chosen. Not only am I giving back, but I am really *giving*, not just doing. I found that if you're patient and keep on looking, you'll eventually find a place where your heart truly belongs, in an organization that feels as though it's tailor-made to your value set and most important beliefs. When you do find that place, you'll feel as though you're receiving just as much as you're giving.

And that's one of the great things about living a life where you're aligned with your values: almost *everything* feels as though it's tailor-made to your most important beliefs and to who you are as a person. Work becomes play, and the moments flow together with ease and grace as you move from one fulfilling activity to the next.

Now that you understand the importance of values, it's time to look at which values you personally hold most near and dear to your heart.

Idea Book Exercise

—Values Clarification—

What you value most will tend to stand out as you read the directory of fifty values below. Put an indication beside each word that resonates with you as you scan down the list. From your notations, select your top ten values, and arrange them in order of importance. If you're having trouble narrowing the list to ten, don't worry: make it your top-twelve or top-fourteen list instead. Also—if you're having trouble prioritizing because, for example, you rate both your spouse and your children as number one, simply have two number ones. You may find that some words on the list seem very similar (ie. happiness and fulfillment); different words evoke different emotions in people, and if you're stuck between two choices that appear to be the same thing, just choose the word that appeals most to you. In addition, there may be values missing that represent an integral part of who you are. Make this list your own, and customize it any way you like.

Values List

Freedom	Friendships
Happiness	Making a difference
Peace of Mind	Spirituality
Fun	Independence
Excitement	Personal Growth
Travel	Creativity
Power	Adventure
Love / Marriage / Relationship	Security

Family	Fulfillment
Respect from others	Knowledge
Courage	Wisdom
Success	Justice
Honesty	Morality
Open-mindedness	Kindness
A sense of humour	Loyalty
Integrity	Community
Career / Job	Generosity
Controlling my own business	Ethics
Empathy	Tolerance
Philanthropy	Service
Retirement	Optimism
Fame	Balance
Health	Authenticity
Confidence	Wealth
Knowing accomplished & successful people	Possessions

It's important to rank your values in order of importance so you have a pre-determined order of operations to follow if your values are ever tested. Imagine, for example, you've listed your job or career as number five on the list and your spouse and kids are tied in the number one spot. If you're constantly being asked to work late or on weekends and end up feeling as though you're never seeing your family, the priority sequence you've chosen will provide clarity and direction to support the decision to make some changes in your life.

Get Noticed. Be Remembered.

My Top 10 Values
in order of importance

1. ....

2. ....

3. ....

4. ....

5. ....

6. ....

7. ....

8. ....

9. ....

10. ....

The Top 5 are your core values.

DATE: _____

Once you've chosen your top ten values, transfer the first five onto the diagram below. The ranking will remain important as a reference if your values are challenged, but you'll notice that it becomes less prevalent on the value map below. This is because the five values you've chosen (your core values) are all interconnected—they're so important to your life that if any one was missing your world would be incomplete. Just as a wheel missing a cog won't turn properly, neither will your circle of meaning if any of the core values are absent. Take heart if some of the core values you've listed are aspirational in nature and haven't happened yet. As long as you have representation in some shape or form of those five core values in your life, you'll feel balanced and fulfilled while you're taking the steps to bring the others to fruition.

Your Core Values

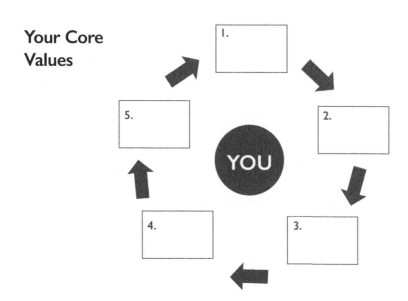

Rocks or Sand?

A philosophy professor stood before his class. Wordlessly, he picked up an empty glass jar and proceeded to fill it with small rocks.

He asked the students if the jar was full, and they agreed that it was.

The professor then picked up a box of pebbles and poured them into the jar. He shook the jar slightly, and the pebbles rolled into the open areas between the rocks. The students laughed.

He again asked his students if the jar was full, and again they agreed that it was.

The professor then picked up a box of sand and poured it into the jar. Of course, the sand filled up the remaining spaces.

"Now," said the professor, "I want you to recognize that this is your life. The rocks are the important things—your family, partner, health, children—anything so important that if it were lost, you would be nearly destroyed.

The pebbles are other things that matter, but on a smaller scale. The pebbles represent things like your job, your house, your car. The sand is everything else. The small stuff.

"If you put sand or pebbles in the jar first, there is no room for the rocks. The same goes for your life. If you spend all of your energy and time on the small stuff, material things, you will never have room for the things that are truly most important."

Pay attention to the things that are critical in your life.

There will always be time to go to work, clean the house, give a dinner party and fix the garbage disposal.

Take care of the rocks first—the things that really matter.

Set your priorities. The rest is just sand.

Learning to

DREAM
ON PAPER

Dreams are...
illustrations from the book
your soul is writing about you.

MARSHA NORMAN

MARTIN LUTHER KING DIDN'T SAY, "I have a goal." Nor did he say, "I have a strategic plan of attack." In his historic and famous speech he said, "I have a *dream!*"

I believe you, too, have a dream. Maybe you can picture it clearly, or perhaps it's locked away deep within your mind. You may even have more than one. Now is the time to set your dreams free.

The key is that you can't just dream in your head. You need to translate your dream into words - on paper. *The most important part of dreaming is writing it down.*

Jim Carrey, one of Hollywood's top actors, experienced first-hand the power of visualization and written goals. Once, when dreaming about becoming a celebrity, he wrote himself a check for $10 million "for acting services rendered" and dated it far into the future. According to his friend Wayne Fleming, he used to keep it in his back pocket, saying, "Someday I'm going to cash that check." A few years later, he was offered the lead role in the movie The Mask. The date on the check in his pocket was almost identical to the date on the film contract, and the dollar value for his part? More than $10 million.

When following up with a client, I asked how her Idea Book was working for her. She replied, "Krista, it's crazy. Whenever I'd mention something I wanted in life you used to say, 'Write it down, write it down!' At the time, it bugged me but I did it anyway, just to humor you. Now I'm almost afraid to write things down because they keep coming true!"

Strange yet wonderful things have happened in my own life as a result of things I've written down. I started my professional organizing business from a phone number for the National Association of Professional Organizers, a number I had written down years earlier. The vehicle parked in my driveway is the same make and model as the photo glued to a page in my coveted notebook. Most recently I was stunned when I realized I was living out my Ideal Day in its entirety — a day I had long ago enshrined in my Idea Book. It's amazing.

After watching how this process had delivered tangible results in my own life, I thought it might be worthwhile to see if it would work for someone else, too. My soul brother Haldon has never been much of a sit-down-and-write-your-goals-out-on-paper kind of guy, but since I'm that type of gal he gradually conceded to at least talk to me about his dreams. Over time he graduated to jotting a few things down in a plain spiral notebook in point form. What I might embellish into a full page he would write as one line in his book, or if he was really feeling expressive, maybe two.

One day I pulled out my Idea Book and started to write down the goals I wanted to accomplish in the coming year. I had a separate section for each type of goal: physical goals, soul goals, financial goals and professional goals. After a while Hal began talking about some of his own goals and aspirations. He wanted a career in sports; in particular, he wanted to work for Hockey Canada. Number two on his list was to work for a professional baseball team. I wrote only seven words in my Idea Book under the heading "Hal" that day, and then closed the book. He later transferred those same words into his own spiral notebook.

Fast forward fourteen months, and the telephone rang. On the other end was an acquaintance Hal met a year and a half earlier when he was chairman of the Air Canada Cup Hockey Tournament. "Hal," he said, "I'm calling to tell you I've emailed you posting and a job description. What would you think about coming to work for us here at Hockey Canada?"

> *You don't have to save everything you write*
> *(in a journal). The benefit is in the process,*
> *The evidence is in your life.*

VICTORIA MORAN

Now it's time to start doing some dreaming of your own (on paper, of course). To help formulate your thoughts, jot down notes while you go through the following exercises. When you feel you have a good handle on your responses, copy the entire exercise into your Idea Book, remembering to put the date at the top of each new entry. You may find it difficult to get started with your Idea Book initially, as well as each time you start a new one after filling an old one. By rewriting your answers to the exercises from this book on the first few blank pages of each new book, you'll have taken some action and removed a bit of the paralysis that comes with attempting to create on a blank canvas. And, if you leave some space at the end of each exercise you allow yourself to add more things as you think of them, freeing you from any perfectionist tendencies that may tempt you to wait until you can get it "right" and "finish it" the first time.

The first exercise is called My Ideal Day and it's one of my favorites. I particularly love reading the Ideal Days of my clients because they're all so different. Some people's Ideal Day is a work day, for others it's a Saturday, and for some it doesn't matter because they see themselves as retired. Perhaps you need to consider two Ideal Days—one for work days and one for holidays.

The key is to be as specific as possible, and to think big. To get your creative juices flowing I've included my own Ideal Day, as written in my Idea Book years ago - the first time I did the exercise. Reading my answer, I can't help but think back to the time I wrote those words. I was working ten to twelve hours a day as the marketing director for a hockey team, driving a little, bare-bones Ford Festiva and living in a rented, very dark two-bedroom basement suite— no French doors or patio terrace there, that's for sure! I hadn't seen the inside of a gym in years, dinner was never homemade unless I went to a friend's place on weekends, and forget reading or going for a walk after my thrown-together evening meal—I could barely muster the energy to drag myself to bed by 11 p.m. each night.

Almost exactly two years from the day I wrote that original Ideal Day, I was laying in bed, winding down my evening when a familiar, almost déja vu feeling came over me. It was as though I had lived this day before.

My Ideal Day   DATE: Sept. 15

Wake up at 6:30 a.m., get dressed into workout gear and
head off to the gym in my silver, fully loaded VW Jetta.
Have a great workout and return to our beautiful four-
bedroom brick home. Go into the spacious, sun-filled
kitchen, prepare breakfast, open the French doors off the
kitchen and sit down to leisurely eat and read the paper
on our patio terrace. Hop into the shower and get
dressed for the day. Go into my home office to check email,
return phone calls, etc. and prepare for the afternoon. Have
a nice relaxing lunch on the patio at a great restaurant with a
friend or a client, and be back in the office by 1:30 p.m. Enjoy
a solid, busy and productive afternoon at the office, shutting
down by about 5:15 p.m. Then put on some comfortable
clothes and great tunes on the stereo to relax and
comfort me. As I start to prepare dinner, my love arrives at
the door with kisses and a gorgeous bundle of fresh
flowers. We cook dinner together and go over our day.
After dinner and dishes are done we go for a walk or just
sit out on the terrace enjoying each other's company.
Reading time is 8 p.m.—we hop under a blanket on the
couch in front of the roaring fireplace to read for almost
an hour. We then prepare for the next day, laying out
clothes, etc. Our evening ends with a quick soak in our
Jacuzzi soaker tub or by making a quick call to a friend. In
bed by 10 p.m., with the candles blown out by 10:45 p.m.

And that was just it—I *had* lived it before—*in my mind*. It was then that I realized I'd just lived out my Ideal Day almost to the letter. A few details were different—I'd driven to the gym that morning in a fully loaded silver SUV instead of a Jetta. The fireplace was gas, and could hardly be described as roaring. There wasn't a Jacuzzi soaker tub in the new townhouse, nor did it have four bedrooms or brick accents. Still, the life I was living was uncannily close to the life I had dreamed up just two years earlier. And then six months later the next move was into—you guessed it—a four-bedroom home complete with brick accents, a Jacuzzi soaker tub in the sprawling 600-square-foot master bedroom, and a roaring wood fireplace in the living room.

This book will show you how I made the jump from my former life to my Ideal Day in two short years. It's about helping you do the same, using the same process I used and many of my clients have gone through in their own personal quests for a more meaningful and authentic life.

Now it's time to roll up your sleeves and start living by design rather than by default. Keep in mind one thing, however: whenever one door closes in life, another one opens. It's important to keep your goals just beyond your reach, and to continually set new goals that cause you to stretch and dream bigger than you ever could imagine. Every six months (or at a minimum once per year), I strongly encourage you to revisit the exercises in this book. Keep your answers fresh and appealing, and adapt to your changing circumstances. You may find certain things you once wanted are no longer a good fit—remove them from your list. You'll also find yourself checking things off your list that you've brought to reality. When that happens, celebrate your victory and then replace those items with brand new ideas. One last point: don't forget to write down your answers (even if it's in point form). Annoying? You bet. But humor me, and then watch the results unfold before your eyes. Happy dreaming!

Idea Book Exercise

— Dreaming on Paper —

My Ideal Day   DATE: _____
Source: *Wishcraft,* Barbara Sher

....
....
....
....
....
....
....
....
....
....
....
....
....

ACTION ITEM: When you've formulated your thoughts in
point form, write the full story of your Ideal Day into your Idea
Book. Remember to be excruciatingly attentive to details when
doing this exercise, writing down what time of day you would
wake up, what you would eat for each meal, the color and
texture of the upholstery in your vehicle (leather or cloth?).
Details, details!

The Unlimited List   DATE: _____
Source: *SuperSelf,* Charles J. Givens

If I had unlimited time, talent, money, knowledge, self confidence
and support from my family, here is a list of everything I would
do with my life:

....
....
....
....
....
....
....
....
....
....
....
....
....
....
....
....
....

ACTION ITEM: Now write your edited Unlimited List into
your Idea Book, leaving an extra page or two at the end so that
as you think of new things, you can add them to the list.

50 Things I Love
(in no particular order)

DATE: _____

1.	20. ....
2.	21. ....
3.	22. ....
4.	23. ....
5.	24. ....
6.	25. ....
7.	26. ....
8.	27. ....
9.	28. ....
10.	29. ....
11.	30. ....
12.	31. ....
13.	32. ....
14.	33. ....
15.	34. ....
16.	35. ....
17.	36. ....
18.	37. ....
19.	38. ....

50 Things I Love (continued)
(in no particular order)

39. ....

40. ....

41. ....

42. ....

43. ....

44. ....

45. ....

46. ....

47. ....

48. ....

49. ....

50. ....

....

....

....

....

....

....

....

....

....

....

ACTION ITEM: Transfer your 50 Things I Love list into your Idea Book, and add another fifty (or more!) blank lines after the list you've already compiled so you can develop and expand your list as you think of new things you love.

Symbols & Songs   DATE: _____

If you could design a logo, or choose an existing symbol that represents your authentic self and/or stands for your best life, what would it be?

....

....

....

....

....

....

....

....

If you could choose one song to be your personal theme song, a song that's lyrics and music speak to your beliefs and philosophy, what song would it be? If you can't find one that fully appeals to you, write your own theme song or compile lines and verses from existing melodies.

....

....

....

....

....

....

....

....

The Awareness of

GOAL
SETTING

A goal without a date is like a check
without a signature. It may have some
value, but don't try to cash it.

JOHN M. RAVAGE

ONCE YOU'VE CLARIFIED YOUR VALUES and done some
dreaming on paper, it's time to move into goal setting. In
this stage you'll be translating the abstract into the concrete,
bridging the gap between fantasy and reality.

When you look at your Ideal Day and your Unlimited
List you'll form a pretty good idea about the basic themes
for your goals. Rather than choosing to work on everything you desire simultaneously, start by going back
through both of those exercises and picking out the must-
have elements in each exercise. This includes those items
you consider indispensable—things without which you
would feel unfinished at the end of your life.

My client, Rob, had the following Ideal Day, Unlimited
List and 50 Things I Love:

Rob's Ideal Day   DATE: Oct 22

I wake up at 6:20 a.m. (my usual time) in the house I designed
on the north side of the San Francisco Bay. It's June 21, the
first day of summer, and the sun is already warm, leaving me
with that wonderfully grateful feeling. I take a moment to take
in the view of the city from the deck outside my bedroom
and then start my exercise routine on the spot.

I carry my breakfast down the covered outdoor steps
that lead from the dining area to the gazebo, which over-
looks my sloping back yard. As usual, my Daytimer is beside
me as I eat my breakfast (fresh orange juice, granola and
English muffins with blackberry jam), so I can go over my
to-do list from last night and make changes or additions that
come to mind.

After breakfast, while everyone else in the Bay Area is in
their car, I stay put and take care of my emails and phone
calls. The biggest item on my list for this morning is planning
an upcoming trip to New York with my little sister, where the
philharmonic will be doing Mahler's Fifth at Carnegie Hall in
a couple of weeks. There's also an email from my neighbors
who are hosting our weekly supper club get-together tonight.
They are convinced I must be lonely, living in this spacious
house all by myself (cat notwithstanding) and thus the email
mentions a friend of Leanne's from work will also be there.
I think it's kind of cute, these well-meaning attempts at fixing
me up with someone.

After an hour of practicing the guitar and the piano in my characteristically haphazard way (playing along with CDs, stopping them when I feel like noodling on my own), it's time to get ready for my downtown lunch date with the owner of the gallery where my show is opening next week. In recognition of the first day of summer, I take the hardtop off Princess Elizabeth, the white 1956 Thunderbird I dreamed of for years and then was lucky enough to acquire. When I designed this house, I made a pact that I would limit myself to four cars, period, but every once in awhile I find some beautiful car somewhere I feel I can't live without and begin making sketches for underground parking spaces under the lower garage; elevators; roundhouses, and all kinds of crazy stuff before finally giving up and making myself stick to my promise.

Lunch is great, gnocchi in pesto and a glass of Bardolino, and the owner shows me the poster for the show—it always tickles me to see my oddball name in print. I pop into a clothing store on my way back to the parkade, and although my Scottish blood sometimes gets in the way, today I splurge and pay full retail for the pants and shirt as I know the upcoming show will probably bring in some good extra money.

Back at home, I put my new things away, throw on some old duds, and head downstairs to the workshop. Today I have to pack a sculpture for shipment to a gallery in Montreal and do some final testing on an Amadeus unit (a high-end home audio system I developed seven years ago after selling my first company). On the way past my little workshop office, I notice an order for two more Amadeus units on the fax machine, and then the phone rings: it's one of the members of my orchestra (the world's smallest— only five musicians!), confirming tomorrow night's rehearsal for our performance of Carmina Burana with the Festival Singers, and some noteworthy soloists, to be held at St. Stephen's (of all places).

After a fabulous meal at Dennis and Leanne's, I walk the hilly two-and-a-half blocks home at a spirited pace. I have a quick stretch before bed, with my Daytimer beside me so I can jot down tomorrow's tasks and see if I have any appointments I may have forgotten. In bed, I glance around the room before nodding off, and kick myself for making it a bit too large, then congratulate myself for having included a fireplace. There are a million lights down the hill and across the bay, but it's wonderfully quiet in my room, and I sleep well.

Rob's Unlimited List DATE: Oct. 25

- start a five-piece orchestra to perform classical works like rock stars
- travel: especially architectural tours
- patent and license numerous inventions
- produce some musical recordings
- start a chain of talking-book radio stations
- support the SPCA
- meticulously restore some vintage electronic equipment
- start an authentic '50s group called the Tru-Tones
- write a book
- go on long driving/photography trips
- design at least one house
- improve my musical skills
- fly to major cities three or four times a year to hear a Mahler symphony
- design my own clothes and have them made for me
- learn how to and then go paragliding
- learn to fly a small plane or helicopter and then buy my own
- make anonymous, surprise gifts to needy people
- restore a couple of old houses to save them from demolition
- make electric sculptures to show and sell in galleries
- develop a convincing Buddy Holly improvisation
- live in a place (or places) where the temperature is always above 10 degrees Celsius

50 Things Rob Loves   DATE: Nov. 7

1. the music of Gustav Mahler
2. warm sunshine
3. maple syrup
4. my special someone
5. my family
6. flying through the air (intentionally)
7. beautifully made furniture
8. beautifully made electronic equipment
9. beautifully made machinery
10. making music
11. listening to music
12. laughter
13. solitude
14. good company
15. feeling healthy
16. seeing my ideas in solid form
17. writing
18. being able to think
19. colors
20. nature
21. biking
22. traveling
23. driving my car
24. riding my bike
25. interesting architecture

26. '50s music
27. good clothes
28. freedom from extraneous noise (people-generated)
29. women
30. unexpected good fortune
31. reading
32. swimming in warm freshwater
33. being appreciated
34. opera rolls (cashews, caramel, nougat)
35. using my hands
36. the aesthetics of the first half of the 20th Century
37. a comfortable bed
38. designing things
39. being near the water
40. a gourmet meal as an occasion
41. romance
42. visiting big cities, especially NYC
43. making people happy
44. scenic highways
45. the smell of cedar trees
46. watching joyful displays of virtuosity
47. unusual humor
48. simple geometrics in natural materials
49. learning about human nature
50. unpretentious jazz

If you want to ensure your goals are propelling you to a balanced life, you can utilize the following categories as headers in your Idea Book, listing your goals in each category:

Physical Goals

Financial

Goals Soul

Goals Family

Goals
Professional Goals

In addition, it's valuable to ask yourself the following questions about each goal:

- How long, realistically, will it take me to accomplish this goal?

- Am I truly committed to achieving it?

- If I had a magic wand and could make this goal happen immediately, would it be something I would really want once I had it?

- Is this an interim goal en route to something greater?

- Is this important in the scheme of my grand vision and overall plan?

- The way this goal is worded, is it specific and concrete?

- Is it measurable?

- How will I know when I've attained it?

When you have a firm handle on your list of goals and have answered each of the questions above for all of them, it's time to do a quick check against your top 10 values to ensure they're aligned. If you're struggling to reach a particular goal, it may be that the goal conflicts with one of your values. For example, if your goal is to make $150,000 this year but your number one value is family, you may have a difficult time, especially if achieving your financial goal means going to work at 7 a.m. and walking in the door, totally exhausted, at 10 p.m.

Take a look at the top ten values for Rob, the inventor:

Rob's Top 10 Values   DATE: Sept. 15

  1. Freedom

  2. Fulfillment

  3. Happiness

  4. Peace of mind

  5. Health

  6. Personal growth

  7. Making a difference

  8. Creativity

  9. Friends

 10. Travel

Thus, his "core values" are as follows:

Rob's Core Values

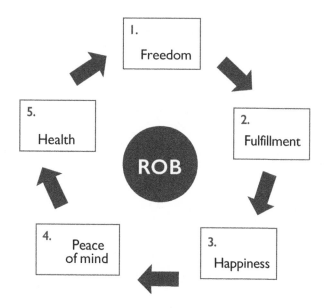

Based on his Ideal Day, Unlimited List and the 50 things he loves, it's pretty easy to see Rob's goals are well aligned with his top ten, as well as his five core values. The way he spends his time and his chosen activities and pursuits all fit with his core brand values. The three elements of clarity, consistency and authenticity are evident.

Once you've compared your list of goals with your values, it's time to do some creative brainstorming. Think about different ways you can achieve each of your goals, letting your imagination run wild. Explore all the traditional routes, and then really push the envelope exploring new ways to make each goal happen. Write down every last idea, regardless of how silly or crazy it seems. Sometimes the wild ideas get the best results. If you're having trouble, ask someone else's opinion. You'll likely get ideas you would never have thought of yourself. For this sort of exercise two heads are indeed better than one.

The Fisherman

A fisherman docked his boat in a tiny, quaint village.

A tourist approached his boat, complimenting the fisherman on the quality of his fish and asked how long it took him to catch them.

"Not very long," answered the fisherman.

"But then, why didn't you stay out longer and catch more?" asked the tourist.

The fisherman explained his small catch was sufficient to meet his family's needs.

The tourist asked, "But what do you do with the rest of your time?"

"I sleep late, fish a little, play with my children, and take a siesta with my wife. In the evenings, I go into the village to see my friends, have a few drinks, play the guitar, and sing a few songs... I have a full life."

The tourist interrupted, "I have an MBA from one of the best business schools in the world, and I can help you! You should start by fishing longer every day. You can then sell the extra fish you catch. With the extra revenue, you can buy a bigger boat. With the extra money the larger boat will bring, you can buy a second one and a third one and so on until you have an entire fleet of trawlers. Instead of selling your fish to a middleman, you can negotiate directly with the processing plants and maybe even open your own plant. You can then leave this little village and move to Mexico City, Los Angeles, or even New York City! From there you can direct your huge enterprise."

"How long would that take?" asked the fisherman.

"Twenty, perhaps twenty-five years," replied the tourist.

"And after that?"

"Afterwards? That's when it gets really interesting," answered the tourist, laughing. "When your business gets really big, you can start selling stocks and make millions!"

"Millions? Really? And after that?"

"After that you'll be able to retire, live in a tiny village near the coast, sleep late, play with your grandchildren, catch a few fish, take a siesta, and spend your evenings drinking and enjoying your friends."

POSITIONING
Your Brand

Choosing the lot and your new neighborhood

Searching for Passion...

AND FINDING IT

I searched endlessly for someone wonderful
who would step out of the darkness and change
my life. It never crossed my mind
that person could be me.

ANNA QUINDLEN

I'M NOT SURE WHEN IT HAPPENED but somewhere along the way, amid the hustle and bustle of life, I lost myself. Growing up I'd always been an enthusiastic, dynamic, positive bundle of energy—but suddenly the sparkle was gone from my eyes and my body felt completely devoid of its high-spirited life force. I'd lost my verve, my zest for life.

It was a year after I'd graduated high school; my twelve month reign as the local pageant winner had just drawn to a close. A career-ending injury forced me to quit competitive figure skating and leave behind a life that had captivated and challenged me since the age of four. For the first time in my life I had no idea who I was or what I should do next.

As I began the search for my authentic self, I began to realize that before I could discover my passion I needed to answer a far more important question: Who am I?

The reason why the world lacks unity, and lies
broken and in heaps, is because man is
disunited with himself.

RALPH WALDO EMERSON

Young children are great at being their authentic selves. They can't help being who they are authentically, because they haven't yet learned to hide behind the social masks so many of us wear. My first logical thought on the path to self-discovery was that I needed to start at the beginning, by going back to the time when all I knew how to be was me.

Fortunately, my mom is uber organized. Flip open the dictionary to the word "organized" and I'm sure her photograph is beside the definition, smiling out from the page to greet you. And, in true Pat Mintern fashion, she'll probably have anticipated your visit and prepared a sandwich for you, too! Considering the meticulous records I had to work with, starting from the beginning wasn't difficult.

My first stop was the photographs. Opening my baby book, I combed through the early years of my life like a detective on a mission. I was looking for clues, anything at all that would tell me what I was like when I was my most authentic self. Who was I, before the world began to tell me who I should be? What was I like as a little person? Happy? Outgoing? Smart? Funny?

The results surprised me. I'd been all of those things— and more. In fact, I'd really been quite an amazing little individual!

The strange thing about completing this exercise was that it was almost like I was talking about someone else when I described myself as a child. Then at some point I realized that this exciting person I was talking about was ME! How I described myself as an adult was very different from the way I described myself as a child—and most of the adult descriptions weren't very positive in nature, either. I decided then and there that my grown-up labels no longer mattered. Who I was on the inside was still the same person I'd been as a child, and the things that had happened to me throughout my lifetime were just that—things that had happened *to* me, not things that *were* me. I firmly believe a person's soul is the one part of them that remains constant over time. As I get older and look in the mirror, it literally astounds me to see signs of age, because on the inside I feel just like I always have.

When I read the book *Mars and Venus on a Date* by John Gray, I came across a passage that supported the very same feelings I'd been experiencing. He articulates it better than I ever could in the following excerpt:

"The soul is that aspect of who we are that is most lasting. On the level of the soul, you are the same throughout your life. The person who was a little child is the same person you are now. The soul is that part of you that doesn't change. The way you physically look, the way you feel, and the way you think about things, however, do change. The most change happens on the physical level. Everything on the physical plane is always changing. As we progress to the emotional plane, we change less. All adults can easily reflect back and still feel many of the feelings they had in childhood or young adulthood. On the mental plane, change is even less.

We tend to be interested in the same sort of things our entire lives. Certainly there is some change, but definitely not as much as on the physical level. On the soul plane we are always the same.

The soul is who you are when you strip away the body, mind and heart. Your soul has a potential that takes an entire lifetime to be fully realized."

After the photographs, I began to look at more tangible items for clues. When I turned 19 my mom gave me a Rubbermaid tote filled with memorabilia—toys, books and other things of mine she'd been saving since I was a baby. Going through that bin, item by item, was an emotional trip down memory lane.

I learned so many things that day. For one, I realized how much I rely on my sense of smell. Opening the tote, one of the first things I found was my old Raggedy Ann doll. Without thinking, I raised it to my nose. One whiff and I felt like I was three years old again. When I told my Mom she laughed. "I know," she said, "you smell everything, and you always have." Later my nieces came over for a visit and this time it was me who laughed: one of them does the exact same thing, too.

I returned to the tote, but this time it wasn't just for the warm fuzzies. My intention was clear: I was trying to find out who I was before the world started to tell me who I should be.

I went through all of my report cards to see what my teachers had said were my strengths and abilities, identifying any patterns that appeared and underlining words consistently used by different teachers. By the time I got to grade ten, I realized the first word on every report card since kindergarten had been the word 'organized'!

It was a haunting moment. I flipped back in my Idea Book and sure enough, as I remembered, there was a phone number for the National Association of Professional Organizers. I had no idea why I'd written it in my notebook at the time—it was just a few words and a phone number casually jotted between a list of books I wanted to read. The more I thought about it, the more signs pointed me in this direction.

I remembered days playing with school friends who had messy homes; I loved going there to play house because it meant I could clean things up and get them organized. When asked about my childhood during a newspaper interview, I suddenly realized that I used to perform a massive overhaul of my closet and the entire contents of my room every six weeks or so, ripping everything apart and redesigning a new and better system for organizing. This was an epiphany for me: I had held the belief that my room had always been messy growing up, but now I instantly understood the psychology behind it—after each of these bedroom "purges" I would have to let it all pile up again over the next six weeks so it was out of control enough to erase the pattern so I could do it all over again!

I spent that night researching. By the next morning I'd decided I would become a Professional Organizer. I'd have to start my own business, because in this early stage of the industry there was no such thing as an employer. And that's how Organized for Life, my first company, was born. It went on to become the first professional organizing franchise system and the industry's first employer, providing opportunities for Professional Organizers to work part-time or without having to open their own business.

I didn't stop with reading just my report cards in my memorabilia tote that day. I kept digging, finding various awards I'd earned in school including an essay contest I'd won and an invitation letter saying I'd been chosen to attend a Young Author's Conference (and the subsequent certificate of completion after I attended). I hadn't remembered either of these things, but once I saw the certificates another memory came flooding back. I remembered the swimming pool in our backyard when I was growing up and how on summer holidays I would lay by the pool, stretched out on the diving board on my stomach with a yellow pad of ruled paper like the kind that writers use, and I would do just that: I'd write. At the time, it was fiction. I would describe the adventures of twin girls who were central characters in all my stories. Never in my adult life had I pondered writing as a career, but here in front of me were clear signs of another forgotten passion — and talent.

> *Seekers are offered clues all the time from the world of the spirit. Ordinary people call these clues coincidences.*
>
> DEEPAK CHOPRA

Leaving my parents house armed with this knowledge, I returned back to my own home and looked around. Suddenly when I was walking past one of the bookcases, my glance fell to the three wicker baskets on the bottom shelf and I gasped, hardly believing what I saw. I pulled them out, lining them up in a row on the floor. Shocked, it dawned on me that the file folders in each of the baskets were more than just a collection of articles and notes. Each folder was a chapter; each basket, a book. I'd thought nothing of this before, other than the inner assumption I'd made that for the past decade and a half I had a weird hobby of collecting strange information that I just couldn't seem to part with. Now I knew why: for the past 15 years, since I was 11 years old, I'd been subconsciously researching and writing a book.

Take a good hard look around your home. Really *see* the things in your office. Go through any childhood memorabilia you can find. Play detective—what you discover may just change your life.

Idea Book Exercise

— Finding Your Passion —

Ask yourself the following questions, and record your answers in your Idea Book to see if you can pick out any patterns and/or trends in the search to find your passion:

1. What were your favorite subjects in school?

2. In which subjects did you have your strongest grades?

3. What did you like best, and what did you like least, about each of the jobs you've held so far?

4. Which job did you prefer most?

5. What type of volunteer activities do you desire most?

6. What tasks have brought you the most success in life?

7. What subjects do you most enjoy reading about?

8. What kind of people do you like best?

9. What are your favorite pastimes or hobbies?

10. When you described your Ideal Day in your Idea Book, what job(s) or occupation(s) did you list?

11. If there weren't any, did you list or describe any type of workplace environment?

12. What is your dream job?

13. Go through any memorabilia you're able to find from your youth and look at it through the eyes of a detective. What conclusions can you draw from the various items?

14. Who do you admire in life, and why?

Finding Your

PLACE IN
THE WORLD

*When people see their own creative power,
they are unafraid to dream, to look beyond personal
limitations, to imagine a new future, to take risks, to
find renewed hope and trust in their own ideas.*

JUDY SEDGEMAN

DETERMINING YOUR PLACE IN THE UNIVERSE is the equivalent
to positioning the Book of You within a bookstore. You're
looking to attract the right audience and to determine
which section best represents your content.

To effectively position your personal brand for maximum
impact, you must abide by the three laws of positioning.
These laws are:

LAW 1: KNOW THY SELF

LAW 2: KNOW THY AUDIENCE

LAW 3: KNOW THY COMPETITION

LAW 1: KNOW THY SELF

In the first phase - Defining Your Brand - we discussed law number one, Know Thy Self. By now you should have a firm grasp on who you are and what you like—your personal preferences. But how do your personal preferences affect your relationships with other people? And what impact do they have on finding your place in the world and determining where you belong?

In the second phase - Positioning Your Brand - the focus shifts from creating the blueprint for your house to determining the neighborhood in which to build it. In terms of your personal brand, this is the equivalent of asking where you want to be positioned in the marketplace.

The first thing to consider is context. You wouldn't build an alpine A-frame in a modern neighborhood, but you *would* want to take advantage of a fabulous downtown view when situating your windows if you had one. In some cases building codes and zoning bylaws restrict what you can do on a particular lot, but the first step always begins with the ideal given the context.

Similarly, many aspects of your personal brand will only become apparent when you've determined your market segment and have some contextual parameters to work with. If your passion is accounting and you like the safety of secure employment, wearing a dark suit and white shirt will probably help you find a career in a large global firm whose corporate culture dictates a conservative dress code. You're unlikely to be hired by a major firm if your authentic personal style includes facial piercings, visible tattoos and a multi-colored, spiked hairdo. But, if you changed the context you could always seek employment in a cutting edge, private company that shares your values and passion for the untraditional.

In the book *Put Your Best Foot Forward*, Jo-Ellan Dimitrius and Mark Mazzarella discuss the importance of physical appearance. Drawing on research collected from thousands of participants, they draw tangible conclusions about the way appearance influences others, causing them to form subconscious biases that affect their actions and alter their decisions. For example, several years ago the New York City Police Department changed the color of their officers' uniforms:

"...from dark blue to light blue in an attempt to reduce the number of assaults on police officers. The theory was that dark blue was an intimidating color which promoted hostile reactions by those who felt threatened by the police. The theory proved true. With the change from dark blue to light blue, the number of assaults on police officers dropped. Unfortunately, police officers complained the public's overall respect also declined, since the light blue uniforms were less authoritarian."

Think of two past American presidents: Bill Clinton and Barack Obama. Their leadership styles were entirely different, and those styles were reflected in their external packaging. We often saw Bill Clinton in jeans and a ball cap, or dressed in casual attire during his presidency. It was unusual to see President Obama, on the other hand, wearing anything but a suit and tie once he got into office. At times you'd see Obama with his jacket off, sleeves rolled up, and tie either loosened or off entirely, but even in those moments he was sending the message that rolling up his sleeves and getting to it was to be done with professionalism and grace. The approach and delivery of each one effectively communicated his value set and determined the positioning of his brand in American society. Obama's more conservative style of dress was consistent with the more stereotypically "Presidential" relationship he had with the American people: personable, yet professional. There was him, and there was us. There was separation between the two. Bill Clinton was positioned much more as "one of us" as if he were an extension of the American people: more like the guy next door. We felt like we knew him. Even the scandal with White House intern Monica Lewinsky felt much more like something that could happen to someone we knew personally rather than POTUS.

As you see with the example above, it's entirely possible for two or more brands to be positioned in the same category or genre with equally effective results, as long as they remain true to their authentic individual style. By being true to who you are, you allow your audience to remain true to who *they* are.

Now it's time to unearth some of the key attributes of your personality, to reveal specific clues as to the best market in which to position your personal brand.

84

Idea Book Exercise

— Place in the World —

In the space provided, write your name. Down the left side of the page, under the "IS" column, write down all of the qualities or words that describe who you are authentically. Add in any characteristics and/or attributes that you may not currently possess but that you aspire to cultivate. Down the right side, under the "IS NOT" column, list any words you feel don't represent who you are now or your future best self, as well as those that go against what you stand for and believe in.

Who Am I?
Source: *Make A Name For Yourself,*
Robin Fisher Roffer

DATE: _____

IS	IS NOT
....	....
....	....
....	....
....	....
....	....
....	....
....	....
....	....
....	....
....	....

Once you have a list that feels accurate and more or less complete, go through the words in the left column and choose the 5 words you feel are the most important to you and best represent what you want to be known for as a human being.

These 5 represent your main "brand attributes" — the key words that you'll now center your personal brand around at all times. These characteristics will set the tone for the development of your external brand packaging and will be reflected in both your signature style and personal marketing materials (which we'll discuss in detail in phase three).

But how do these key attributes affect the positioning of your personal brand? They help you determine the most intuitively "right" niche market in which to position yourself - an environment that nurtures and supports you on all levels. The following is my own "IS" and "IS/NOT" list:

Who Am I	DATE: Feb. 18
IS	**IS NOT**
Authentic	A mathematician
Energetic	Inexpensive
Dynamic	Complacent
International	Prescription writer (surface)
Creative	One who settles
A visionary	Always on time
Professional	Dependent on others
Inspiring/motivating	An extrovert

IS	IS NOT
Honest	Fake or phony
Positive, an optimist	A small-town business
Based in Integrity	Impersonal in my approach
Ambitious	A backstabber
Organized	Tolerant of those who lie
Intelligent	Better than anyone else
A storyteller	Stuck up or unapproachable
Innovative	Argumentative
Customized solutions	Living in my comfort zone
Original	Malicious or vindictive
A premium brand	Satisfied being less than my best
Goal-oriented	A one-project-at-a-time person
A dreamer, believer	One to make excuses

Take a look at the list of brand attributes (the "IS" list) that you've chosen to represent your personal brand. Are there words you've used that indicate a certain market positioning? For example, let's look at the list of my brand attributes above. Some of the "positioning indicators" — those words that may reveal clues to my authentic market segment are:

International	Innovative
High Quality	Premium ("NOT" inexpensive)
Professional	("NOT" an extrovert)
Positive	("NOT" a small-town business)

From this, we can draw the conclusion that the market best suited to my own personality would be a diverse environment filled with positive, professional people who are "outside-the-box" thinkers (but from whom I can take a break now and again to recharge). I'd likely travel and have clients willing to pay a premium for the high quality work I perform. When reviewing your brand attributes and determining your own positioning strategy, ask yourself these three questions:

Where do I want to compete?

What am I best suited for?

What type of people do I most enjoy dealing with?

There are many different markets in which to position your brand, just as there are many different sections of a bookstore and neighborhoods in which to live.

Below is a list of many of those different areas; you can choose one, or combine them for the best fit. In many cases your initial gut reaction will give you a pretty good idea of the best market for your personal brand.

Market segments for positioning your brand

Premium/High-end

Economy/Value

Professional

Casual

Alternative

Family-oriented

Lifestyle-oriented

Career-oriented

You can easily combine your brand to fit into a Premium/ Professional/Career-oriented category, or perhaps a Casual/Professional/Lifestyle-oriented market segment. In the former, you'd probably be dressed in a tailored suit, conducting business in a corporate boardroom; in the latter, you'd likely be casually dressed, conducting business on the golf course. The key is to position yourself in an area that suits you. You want to feel comfortable: not as though you're pretending to be someone—or something—you're not. You must also consider your core brand values—if they're not aligned with the category or market segment you've chosen you'll feel unhappy and unfulfilled, as though you're spinning your wheels.

If you decide your personal brand's positioning strategy is the Premium/Professional/Career-oriented category, for example, but your number one value is your family, you'll be in conflict emotionally. Not only will you feel torn each time you miss your child's dance recital to work late, you'll also feel tormented spending time with your family while still trying to compete with the other high-rollers at the office. The good news is you *can* achieve balance—have your cake and eat it, too—by positioning yourself to reflect your core values. If you were to position yourself as a Family-oriented/Premium/Professional, it'd be clear to those around you that you want to work hard and earn a lot of money, but not at the expense of your family's well-being.

LAW #2: KNOW THY AUDIENCE

As a Family-oriented/Premium/Professional you can use family values as a competitive advantage. Let prospective clients know your family is important to you, and that you want to deal with people who feel the same way.

Treat your clients as members of your business family. Tell them you want to grow and succeed with them. Let them know you're committed to developing a long-term relationship, and you're available from 9 a.m. to 5 p.m. (or whatever your desired work hours might be). Explain to them that you need this balance so you can give your best to both your business and your personal "families."

By doing this, you'll attract family-first clients who are supportive rather than annoyed when you pass on scheduling meetings during non-traditional business hours. Because you've positioned yourself this way, your clients know up front how you operate. They know what they're buying into. There are no surprises later on, and you'll have earned their respect from the get-go.

This modus operandi commands deep loyalty among your followers, with the side benefit of getting people talking about you and your services. It's untraditional and it's gutsy, but it's honorable. That's an unbeatable combination in most people's books, and your client list will reflect that.

The key is to showcase what you really want. Ensure your marketing materials, external packaging and other facets of your image reflect your authentic self and your goals. These items, if reflective of your true inner essence, will work on your behalf to attract like-minded individuals to your personal brand. These are the people who will ultimately support and promote your brand best, because they resonate and connect with it on multiple levels. Whether you're developing your brand for personal reasons or for business purposes, your desired target audience is made up of individuals that we'll call your "Ideal Clients."

When attempting to determine what an Ideal Client might look like, start by thinking about the people who currently form your personal and professional networks. Ask yourself:

☐ What kind of people are they?

☐ What do they think, feel and believe about me (or my products/services)?

☐ What do I want them to think, feel and believe?

☐ What key thought can I put into their minds to achieve that?

☐ Who is competing for their attention and/or loyalty?

☐ Which of them are most profitable? (If you're focusing on your personal life, think about the emotional profit or return on investment)

☐ Why are they profitable? By volume, or profit margin per sale? (Is it an emotional profit based on quantity of time spent together or quality time?)

With a list of your existing audience or current clients in front of you, scan each name and highlight your favorite clients. You know the ones: in a personal capacity they're the people you look forward to seeing again— those men and women who uplift, inspire and challenge you, and make you feel great each time you see them. In a professional capacity they're the clients who pay their bills on time and don't squabble about the price—the ones you pick up and answer the phone instead of letting it go to voicemail. They're the people with whom you thoroughly enjoy the entire experience when dealing with them.

As you scan the list of highlighted names, look for patterns. Are they mostly men? Women? Do they live in a similar geographic area? Do you have a common hobby, occupation, or interest?

The more demographic and psychographic information you can gather, the better. Here are some examples of information that may be helpful:

Demographics

Sex

Age

Culture/Ethnicity

Marital Status

Household size

Occupation

Home owner vs. renter

Income

Religion

Psychographics

Values

Personality type

Introvert vs. Extrovert

Doer vs. Thinker

Positive vs. Negative

Big picture vs. Details

Hobbies

Choices

Personal Style

In addition, individual preferences will often play a role in determining the types of people you like to surround yourself with. These come in the form of common interests and similar likes or dislikes, as a segment of their psychographic profile.

Habits & Preferences

- What books do they read? Magazines? Newspapers?
- TV channels and shows?
- Radio stations?
- What type of vehicle do they drive?
- Favorite retail store(s)?
- Where do they live?
- What restaurants do they frequent?
- What music do they listen to?
- What type of movies do they watch? On DVD, Netflix, or at the theater?
- What do they like to do in their spare time? What are their hobbies?
- Do they travel? Aspire to? If so, what destinations?

From the profile you've gathered, there's a good chance you've come up with a mix of demographics and psychographics to describe your Ideal Client. Now look for any gaps between the profiles of your favorite clients and the bulk of your clients — the names you chose to highlight versus the ones you didn't. Can you see a way to turn someone that isn't currently on the list of your Ideal Clients into one? Does understanding who your Ideal Clients are help you to see how you can attract more of them? Can you see ways in which you can directly market to that type of person?

We've now covered the first two laws (Know Thy Self and Know Thy Audience). The third and final law is to Know Thy Competition. Once you've determined what your brand stands for and who your Ideal Client is, you can now take a look at the competitive landscape to see who else is competing for your target audience's attention.

LAW #3: KNOW THY COMPETITION

From the moment I was born I've been in a hurry. I came into this world faster than my Mom could check into the hospital—I was delivered in the waiting room as she was wheeled in from the parking lot. I walked at eight months old. I started kindergarten a year early and knew by age four what one of my life's passions would be. My Mom took me to an ice show that year, and I sat in utter awe watching figure skater Karen Magnussen perform. As the last note of music sounded and she struck her finishing pose, I looked at my Mom with fire in my young eyes and said, "I want to do that." Every day for the next nineteen years I worked toward that goal.

I rose up the ladder quickly in the figure skating world and before too long was noticed on the regional scene. This ensured I was invited to all the best skating seminars in my area, and that in turn meant exposure to high-level coaches, judges, trainers and sports psychologists.

I was blessed with ample talent in the areas of technical merit and artistic impression, the two categories in which a figure skater is judged in competition. When used properly it was a lethal, and often unbeatable combination. At the age of ten I attempted my first triple jump, and by the time I hit twelve, I was cocky as hell on the ice. But I wasn't taking home very many gold medals.

I read a quote somewhere and even back then it resonated enough for me to have written it down, although I didn't record the source:

Champions don't become champions when they win an event but in the hours, weeks, months and years they spend preparing for it.

UNKNOWN

What I didn't realize was that a large part of my skating success was due to the talented coaches my parents had surrounded me with at such an early age. These trainers had built me into a strong skater—it had far less to do with my raw talent. I know this because in competition, when I was out there all alone on the ice, I was scared. And it showed: I wasn't winning.

Put me in a practice rink in comfortable attire, crank the tunes, and I was in my element, truly unstoppable. But take me out of that environment and whisk me into the competitive arena and I folded like a cheap suit.

One simple reason: I hadn't yet learned to play the game.

When I walked into the arena at my first major competition, I felt as though I'd been punched in the gut. "What happened to the lines on the ice? They're gone!" I hissed under my breath to my coach. Until then I'd always practiced in hockey arenas and was used to the center line, blue lines and face-off circles painted on the ice.

"Welcome to the world of competitive figure skating," she said. "Now you're playing in the big leagues." In other words, you're no longer half hockey player, sista. It's time to see what you can do without the aid of peripheral guides and mental markers! Not only does this mess you up in terms of where to place each jump and spin, but when the lines are gone it becomes blatantly obvious to the judges if your routine is unbalanced. The marks your blades cut into the ice form a distinct pattern and if you haven't covered most of the surface by the end of your program, you're toast.

Nervous about the lack of lines on the ice, I entered the dressing room and found a seat between two big-city skaters who trained at a high-end winter club. Everything about them screamed snooty. They hardly skipped a beat before launching into psychological warfare.

"I'm so nervous," one drawled. "My triple toe-loop has been giving me so much trouble this week." "That's too bad," replied the other one. "I've really peaked at the right time. My triple loop has been my best jump lately!"

Triple toe-loop? Triple loop? Holy smokes, was I in trouble—and we hadn't even laced up our skates! Little did I know that neither of these girls were anywhere near to landing triple jumps—it was just a game to psych out the other skaters. And in my case they were entirely successful, long before we had even stepped onto the ice.

I learned an important lesson that day, one that stuck with me and has served me well in sport, life and business ever since: *Always do your market research.*

I could've done a lot of things ahead of time to prepare for that competition. Had I done so, the results might have been very different. I could have:

- ☐ Investigated the arena where the competition was held. Found out the size of the ice surface and the layout of the stands

- ☐ Practiced my program from both ends in my home rink, and become so proficient at it both ways that which end to start at wasn't an issue

- ☐ Worked on my program, with the music, on the floor and on the ice so that my body and mind went into autopilot mode when the first beat played, allowing me to concentrate on performing

- ☐ Drawn out my routine on paper to see the pattern and ensure that it was balanced

- ☐ Worked on utilizing points on the boards rather than dots and lines painted on the ice for markers when doing jumps and spins

- ☐ Read skating magazines and newsletters and charted what the other skaters were doing and where they were placing in competitions. Learned which technical elements medalists did and did not complete in each category

By doing some legwork, I could've saved myself a lot of heartache and frayed nerves, and may have even hit the ice brimming with confidence, rather than being totally defeated before I started.

The same principles apply when competing in a sport, in business, or as an individual. Do your homework, and pay attention when you're vying to be noticed amongst all the other faces in the crowd!

PUTTING IT ALL TOGETHER

Now that you've chosen the market you'd like to be positioned in, you can begin to define your brand's direction by writing a personal mission statement. This is a concise description of what your life stands for — your highest ideals. It should be fairly broad and general in scope, yet focused on your brand attributes and aligned with your core brand values. It'll be a clear declaration of where you're headed — think of it as your North Star during times of turbulence and uncertainty. Your mission statement is the expression of how you'd like to be remembered at the end of your life.

In his book *First Things First*, Stephen Covey and his co-authors describe a personal mission statement as not only a life guide, but also as an important principle in time management. Their reasoning is simple: if you know what's ultimately important to you, you'll manage your time better to reflect those priorities. Covey says a personal mission statement is a concrete method for "connecting with your own unique purpose and the profound satisfaction that comes in fulfilling it."

If you find it difficult to get started on developing your personal mission statement, I've included a couple of different methodologies to get the brainwaves flowing:

- Covey suggests visualizing your eightieth birthday or fiftieth wedding anniversary and imagining what your friends and family would say about you

- If you're comfortable with your own mortality, you can try writing your own obituary, including what you accomplished, what you stood for, what you believed and what type of person you were

I use a similar exercise (below) with my clients, although it's worded a bit differently and starts with a visualization. Try theirs - or mine - whichever resonates most with who you are. When you have a draft, copy it into your Idea Book.

Imagine you're one hundred years old, sitting in a comfortable chair in front of a beautifully set dinner table. A roaring fireplace warms the room like a thick wool sweater, and soft music plays in the background. The smell of warm apple pie wafts in from the kitchen. You're surrounded by your descendants and the people you care about the most. As you stand to speak, a loving silence fills the room. You begin to tell the story of your life...

Idea Book Exercise

— Place in the World —

If you were to tell the story of your life what wisdom would you impart? What would you say is important in life? Capturing the essence of who you are in your most authentic core, how would you describe your beliefs and accomplishments? Write your answer in the space below.

My Life Story   DATE: _____

Keeping your notes from the Life Story exercise in mind, go through your Idea Book and reflect on the other exercises you've completed. To form a rough draft of your personal mission statement (any length), review the following items:

> Your list of Core Values
>
> Your 50 Things I Love list
>
> Your "Unlimited" list
>
> Your Ideal Day
>
> Your list of brand attributes ("IS" and "IS NOT")
>
> Your Life Story

This isn't a job description. It should be more like a manifesto, a declaration of your highest ideals, a statement about who you want to be and what you want to do in your ideal life. Re-draft this statement every couple of weeks until each statement feels just right. You'll know when it's complete: each word will inspire and motivate you. You'll feel as though you've captured the essence of who you are. It'll reflect your strongest beliefs, hopes, dreams and principles.

Personal Mission Statement

My mission is to live authentically, with integrity, honesty and strength of character. My signature is my smile and I exude radiance, charm and optimism from my lean and healthy body. I love and am loved deeply by those with whom I've chosen to share my life, and I am happy, fulfilled, energetic and original.

Similarly, you might want to formulate a mission statement for your business if you're self-employed. It should reflect your personal goals and the ideals you'd like to see achieved during the company's lifetime. My primary business is guided by a mission that has emerged from my own personal quest for excellence.

Business Mission Statement

I strive to empower my clients to live their best lives daily and work toward the practice of greatness, even when no one's watching. I am passionately dedicated to helping individuals realize their full potential as human beings, not just as humans doing; to unabashedly express their inner essence and bring to the world that which makes them great.

Regardless of the amount of detail you choose to put into your mission statement or its length, it must have soul. It needs to be something that you won't need to memorize in order to recite— you know it by heart because you believe every word.

Idea Book Exercise

— Place in the World —

After you've formulated your notes and ideas in the space below, transfer the first draft of your written personal mission statement into your Idea Book. Keep working on it until each word and each sentence feels exactly right. Your mission statement is something that you'll want to paste where you can see it often, perhaps even framed and hanging on a wall in your home or office.

Personal Mission Statement

PACKAGING
Your Brand

Building your home: furnishing, decorating & landscaping

An Introduction to

PERSONAL STYLE

If you have anything really valuable to
contribute to the world, it will come through the
expression of your personality, that single spark of
divinity that sets you off and makes you
different from every other living creature.

BRUCE BARTON

THERE ARE MANY INTANGIBLES that affect the development of your personal style. Your external presence as a human being, along with the external packaging of your personal brand both contribute heavily. Equally important are your inner traits—characteristics such as discipline and focus. Last (but certainly not least) is the relationship you have with your inner self—your "self-talk"—which affects your confidence, body image and the way you move through the world. These four elements—external presence, external packaging, inner traits and self-talk—are interconnected. Combined, they help to form your personal brand image which influences how others perceive you.

When developing your own signature style, you need to consider all four areas individually. In the pages ahead you'll do this by splitting them into two parts: your inner self and your outer self. But first we need to discuss the importance of making a strong first impression. In a first meeting, all the internal and external manifestations of your personal brand blend together to make that all-important initial impact.

FIRST IMPRESSIONS

Upon first meeting, we judge people based on physical appearance, whether we intend to or not. Many studies have been done on the subject, especially in the area of recruiting and hiring practices, and although many employers *insist* their decisions aren't based on appearance, the findings show otherwise. According to Tanya S. Rosenblat of Wesleyan University:

> "Surprising economic relevance of physical attractiveness is by now a well documented fact. In addition to recent work in economics, research in social psychology, sociology, and human resource management firmly established that good-looking people have significant advantages in negotiation, interviewing, receiving job offers, retaining jobs and being promoted. While experimental studies in economics and social psychology confirm the impact of physical appearance on wages and bargaining power, they cannot explain the origin of such discrimination. These origins might be considered under two potential hypotheses: a) good-looking people do better because interviewers and clients enjoy their physical appearance, and/or b) good-

looking people are in fact more qualified because their physical appearance has previously helped them obtain better skills through the utilization of more extended social networks."

In a related study of electoral voting patterns, the results were clear: the better-looking candidates received an average of two hundred and fifty per cent more votes than the less attractive candidates, yet seventy three per cent of those who cast their votes in the elections resolutely denied that appearance played any role. This is not to say you must be drop-dead gorgeous to be classified as good-looking. How you present yourself in terms of grooming, wardrobe, confidence and carriage all form an image of physical attractiveness. When meeting someone for the first time, several things combine to form a first impression about you:

Handshake

Personal introduction or elevator speech
(a succinct bite of information, thirty words or less)

Eye contact

Body language

Facial expression

Voice

Personal image

What conclusions do you draw in your own mind, based on the first impressions others leave? You can get a good feel for how you judge others, and how people may be judging you, by paying close attention to the way you would answer the following questions after meeting someone new:

- ☐ What did the person's non-verbal communication style say about him or her?

- ☐ What assumptions did you form based on that?

- ☐ In the elevator speech, did the person effectively convey his or her area of specialty and succinctly express the gist of what he or she does?

- ☐ Did the individual ask you to imagine something, show you how he or she can help you, or explain how to solve a problem for you?

- ☐ Did the person utilize a company tagline or tell you any part of their company's story/history?

- ☐ What does the person's business card say about him or her?

I firmly believe everyone should have a personal business card. This includes retirees, stay-at-home parents, students and CEOs. It's a declaration of esteem, as well as an information tool. Elaborate or simple, a personal business card doesn't have to be expensive, nor do you need to print 1,000 at a time. An example of a basic personal business card for someone not affiliated with a company is:

JOHN SMITH

---

123 Any Street
Anytown, Anywhere
Country, Zip Code

Phone: 123-4567
E-mail: info@anyemail.com

If you work for a company that's not your own, it's unlikely that you'll have much say regarding the business card design and print quality. If you're self-employed, however, you have full control and should exercise every ounce of it. Business cards will make a first impression on your behalf if you're utilizing your networks to promote your services, or if you regularly send out packages or proposals to prospective new clients. You have an opportunity for your card to make a bold initial statement about you and your company and give you a huge opportunity to get noticed and be remembered, even if most of your new business comes from existing customer referrals or you're part of an industry where even *having* business cards is untraditional.

An agency called Rethink utilized this unorthodox approach and came up with a great idea for an effective business card card for one of their clients who was a carpenter. They got a simple rubber stamp made with his name and phone number on it, took sheets of low-grade sandpaper and had them professionally cut down to business card size, and then stamped his info onto the smooth (back) side. Voila! He now had a simple, inexpensive yet outrageously effective tool that not only created a strong first impression but got people talking about him and his services (even here - years later - in a book).

Another key to creating a strong first impression is the manner in which you introduce yourself. Whether in a one-on-one situation or in a group setting, your introduction tells your audience who you are. Think about your "elevator speech" ahead of time. Designed properly, it can be delivered to an employer or the client of your dreams in the time it takes to ride an elevator from the first to the top floor. It gives people a succinct and confident run-through of who you are and what you have to offer.

I don't think I fully understood just how powerful an effective elevator speech could be until I was speaking at a lunch event when a dynamic woman stood up and took to the floor to introduce herself. With a warm smile, she said:

"I'd like to invite you to close your eyes for just a moment; take a deep breath, and get quiet. Now imagine for a moment what it would be like to have a partner in your life whose sole purpose is to help you identify and achieve your goals, maximize your potential and maintain healthy balance. Just *imagine* what it would be like to have a partner like that. Now open your eyes. My name is Anita Bakker, and my company is called Essentials for Excellence. I'm an executive coach, and I would love to be that partner in your life."

Pretty powerful stuff amidst a crowd of people repeating "Hi, my name is Bob and I'm a realtor," or similarly traditionally ineffective introductions, right? Get noticed. Be remembered!

Idea Book Exercise

— Personal Style —

Write down the following questions, along with your answers, in your Idea Book.

First Impressions   DATE: ———————————

How does your first impression either contribute to, or contaminate, your personal brand image?

Does it positively or negatively impact the experience someone has with your brand?

Exploring Your

INNER
SELF

*A mode of conduct, a standard of courage,
discipline, fortitude and integrity can do a
great deal to make a woman
(or man) beautiful.*

JACQUELINE BISSET

ELEGANCE IS AN ATTITUDE, and fashion is so much more
than just the clothes you wear. *How* you wear them is as
important as what you wear. That how comes from the
inside—in the form of your confidence, energy and the
relationship you have with your inner self. Five main areas
contribute to your personal brand internally:

ORIGINALITY

ATTITUDE

MOTIVATION
BODY / SELF IMAGE
DISCIPLINE & CHOICES

As you begin to build trust and develop a strong relationship with your inner self, you'll find it becomes easier to be alone with your thoughts without having to fill the silence with external distractions. "Getting quiet with yourself" will take on a new meaning. Just as two friends can sit in silence and then walk away feeling as if it was the best conversation they've ever had, you too will be able to find comfort and security in your own company. As Marcel Marceau once said, "the most moving moments of our lives find us all without words." This compassion and quiet love of self not only inspires trust within yourself but compels others to trust you as well.

Confidence implies assurance, and assurance implies security. If others feel safe around you, they'll open their hearts to you. Your brand's reputation will soar — you'll become known for this without others even being able to articulate what they get from being in your presence.

Never dismiss your inner voice; it's that
'mere feeling' that protects your essence and
propels you towards true fulfillment.

MARCIA BRODSKY

As your reliance on your inner self grows, your intuition will begin to exert itself more strongly. Your intuition operates much like a muscle: the more you exercise it, the stronger it becomes (and the more it can tell you).

Powerful intuition is yet another benefit of improved self-trust. Gaining strength in this area begins by turning down the volume and exploring the silence.

There are a number of vehicles that will enable you to channel the silence within yourself. Some people find inner strength is best gained through quiet pursuits such as yoga or meditation; others find stillness in nature; a large number of people find it through worship. In my view, it matters less how you go about finding it than devoting time each week to searching for it.

Religions are like airlines. They may all have different names, different foods, different seats... but they're all taking you to the same destination.

JOHN EDWARD

Whether you're spiritual, religious, agnostic or atheist is irrelevant—you have an inner voice. I'm sure you've heard it. Perhaps it comes in the form of your conscience, or maybe it's appeared as your inner critic. Positive or negative, naysayer, whisperer or raging tyrant, it's in there. One of the ways you can manage your inner critic is to simply let it be heard. Many times that means slowing down. You need to get quiet for an extended period of time on a regular basis in order to really listen to what it has to say.

Our lives are busy and filled with sensory stimuli. It's no wonder many of us are disconnected from ourselves. It's tough to hear the whisper of your inner voice above all the noise and distractions of the day. Perhaps you need to set aside one day a week (more likely one hour) to pay tribute to some spiritual reflection. This can be done in a religious context, or just by searching the silence for your inner voice.

For me, nature elevates my soul and helps connect me to my spirit. As mentioned earlier, one of my favorite ways to get quiet is to sit behind the wheel on a long stretch of highway, listening to soothing music. With practice, you'll begin to learn what method works best for you. The key is to find a way to get out of your steady thought-stream: to go into a place of deep, effortless concentration. When you find your inner voice, it'll be as though the blinders have been taken off. You'll be greeted with a new understanding of what you believe to be true and real and right in the world—a new sense of your own personal truth.

No man can produce great things who
is not thoroughly sincere in dealing
with himself.

JAMES RUSSELL LOWELL

The only thing more beautiful than raw truth is sharing it with others. When your life is guided by the truth as you see it, you'll be stronger as a human being, and your personal brand will shine from within. But be aware—many truths exist. Truth is based upon individual perception. We give the world our view from the mountaintop, a view shaped by who we are and where we come from. Your view is a unique perspective of the landscape. And others have their own unique perspective, too. It's always helpful to check in with people you love and trust and see if who you believe yourself to be is consistent with what's being communicated through your personal brand. As John Keats wrote, "Beauty is truth, truth beauty—that is all ye know on earth, and all ye need to know."

117

Idea Book Exercise

— Inner Self —

Write down the first ten words or phrases that come to mind when you answer this question, and record these in your Idea Book. Then rank them in order of importance. Any surprises?

The Whole Truth   DATE: _____

What does the word truth mean to you?

ORIGINALITY

It's difficult for me to understand how some people can survive in the world pretending to be someone they're not. I find it ironic that we spend the first half of our lives trying so hard to fit in, and the last half trying to make ourselves stand out. If only someone had sat us down when we were young and told us we could eliminate the heartache of adolescence if we would just listen to our inner selves, if we could let ourselves be, on the outside, a reflection of who we are on the inside. That is the true measure of success.

> *The universe is not going to see someone*
> *like you again in the entire*
> *history of creation.*

VARTAN GREGORIAN

Study a leader who inspires and draws other people into his or her wake. Chances are good this person's popularity doesn't come from copying what others are doing or wearing. It's far more likely that the magnetism they exude comes from having the inner confidence and strength of character to be different, and by having the integrity that inner and outer self-alignment brings.

But what if inner confidence and strength of character are missing from your life? There are a variety of reasons why, over the years, you may have gradually lost ground a little bit at a time. And it may be only now that you're beginning to realize just how much ground you've lost.

You've undertaken much of the process of self-discovery already through the exercises in this book. It's likely that your answers will have revealed many forgotten passions and

---

truths—the things that make you truly unique. In the land of marketing, we call it your USP, or "Unique Selling Point." It's what separates you from your competition, whether it's an actual fact or a perceived specialty. Having a unique vision allows you to move beyond any evolutionary obstacles to forge new paths and bring new ideas to the world. Let's use Hugh Hefner as an example. He once said, "I never intended to be a revolutionary. My intention was to create a mainstream men's magazine that included sex in it. That turned out to be a very revolutionary idea."

By doing what you love and following your passion, the byproduct can sometimes be a concept that has never, or rarely, been done before.

Your life has been a journey; look back at the path you've traveled to get to where you are today. The major milestones you've achieved, the important decisions you've made, the people you've met: each one represents a thread in the fabric you've woven into the beautiful tapestry of your life. It's a pattern that's original to you, and only you. No other human being will ever duplicate your experience on this planet. Utilize the power of being a true original to design a life and a personal brand that reflects your unique personality and skill set.

ATTITUDE IS EVERYTHING

Even if every day is a battle, your attitude has the power to win the war. Attitude is one of the most visible aspects of your personal brand. It determines how you handle adversity, deal with challenges and acknowledge your accomplishments. In other words, it sets the tone for who you are. It may at times be repressed, but it cannot be hidden. Your attitude directly influences people's impression of you.

You might be rolling your eyes right now, thinking, "Oh great, here's where we get the 'don't worry, be happy' speech about positive thinking." Not really. Hear me out.

Your living is determined not so much by what life brings to you as by the attitude you bring to life; not so much by what happens to you as by the way your mind looks at what happens. Circumstances and situations do color life but you have been given the mind to choose what that color shall be.

JOHN HOMER MILLER

There are times when the last thing you want (or need) is to be positive. Being positive is not always the best solution. Sometimes when you're hurting inside it's tough to put on a happy face. As Susan Jeffers writes, "I feel like someone has thrown me in the water to teach me how to swim. Maybe later I'll be thankful for the opportunity. Now, I simply feel like I'm drowning." Sometimes being positive and happy merely glosses over your pain, pushing it down into a temporary hiding place.

So rather than just "thinking positive," try feeling every emotion you experience when going through a hard time. If you've been hurt, be compassionate and give yourself permission to mourn. For example, if you're in the running for a big promotion at work and it's given to someone else, allow yourself to be disappointed (behind closed doors), and work through the emotions you're experiencing.

Consider these words of wisdom from Buddhist teacher Pema Chodron, from the book *The Places That Scare You*:

121

"If you stay and discover the things in yourself that you've always run from, you begin to have some tenderness for your own situation. You're willing to make friends with yourself, in the way that you know everything about a true friend and you still love them. This complete friendship with yourself is the core of any spiritual growth."

A fine line exists, however, between mourning a hurt and wallowing in pain. When your raw emotion loosens its grip, you need to look for what's hidden within the story. Adversity will often have within it a precious seed of wisdom. Many times it'll be a lesson that blooms most fully in time — richer in retrospect than it is in original view.

After you've dealt with the heartbreak of the lost opportunity, go back out there, congratulate your co-worker, and move on. When you release your emotional attachment to the outcome, you'll begin to see in time that even the most disastrous events have been a necessary step in the journey of your life. It's difficult to be patient when things aren't going your way, but if you stay the course and remain focused, the world will find a way to give you what you want. Reflect on this poetic prose by Czech poet Rainer Maria Rilke from the book *Letters to a Young Poet*:

"Have patience with everything unresolved in your heart and try to love the questions themselves as if they were locked rooms or books written in a very foreign language. Don't search for the answers, which could not be given to you now, because you would not be able to live them. And the point is, to live everything. Live the questions now. Perhaps then, someday far in the future, you will gradually, without even noticing it, live your way into the answers."

I've talked a lot about the importance of wearing your heart on your sleeve and about being authentic. I'm convinced this attitude will change your life, especially when helping you cope with adversity. How you deal with challenges - whether the death of a loved one, the loss of a job, or even a string of tangled Christmas lights - says volumes about you as a human being, and even more about your personal brand.

One day I was walking down the street and noticed a homeless man on the sidewalk. His clothes were dirty and torn, yet he was smiling from ear to ear. When I looked at his sign, my eyes filled with tears. Scrawled across the cardboard were words I'll never forget: "$2 short of taking over the world." That's what this book is all about—attempting to be remarkable in everything you do. To be an original. To get noticed and be remembered (in a good way), in a way that not only represents but celebrates who you are and who you're becoming with each new day.

Time continually changes us; each second that passes is now behind us. The key is to realize that the past does not define us—unless we let it. Personal branding is a means of consciously defining and shaping change. Because you've always done something a certain way doesn't make it the best way or the only way. Reach out. Try new things. Be horrible at them, or succeed—it doesn't much matter. You're better for trying, regardless of the outcome.

MOTIVATION

People are motivated in many different ways, but the source of lasting inspiration is always the same: it must come from within. Former Philadelphia Flyers coach Fred Shero nailed it when he said, "Success is not the result of spontaneous combustion. You must set yourself on fire." I agree, Fred.

All it takes is one match to light a forest fire.

ANONYMOUS

Use whatever method or inspiration works for you. Part of your personal brand is based on how you convince yourself to push past your limits in the pursuit of greatness. Some things are easy to do; they flow and they naturally feel simple and effortless to accomplish. I'm not talking about those things. What I'm talking about are those commitments we've made to ourselves regarding things we want to do, but that are anything BUT easy. Those things we know will serve us and move our life forward but that require us to dig in and find new levels of grit and perseverance in order for us to complete.

In my own life, I found a new source of motivation after reading an article in *O Magazine* and visiting Oprah's website (www.oprah.com). I downloaded a copy of a personal contract she'd signed with herself to help her reach her weight loss goals. It sounded intriguing, so I printed it off and started reading. When I got to the end, I'd found some new insight into my own motivational style.

For years, I'd struggled with the notion that if I dangled some form of a carrot just beyond my grasp it would excite me enough to get the job done. But I always ended up failing miserably, whether it meant promising to write five hundred words each morning but never opening my laptop, or falling off a new eating plan by 5pm on the same day I started.

Then, along came the notion of a personal contract. I wrote one, using Oprah's as inspiration but tailoring it to fit my own life. It read:

I, Krista, hereby commit to 6 weeks of intense work on my book, physical exercise, and self control when it comes to eating. This includes fully finishing the entire manuscript of book one and delivering it to my editor no later than June 25. In addition, this includes approximately one hour of exercise six days per week where I'm focused on challenging my abilities and elevating my physical performance. I will endeavor to be conscious of when and why I eat and will, to the best of my ability, simply eat to satisfy my nutritional needs as opposed to my emotional needs. I will also make an effort to make healthful food choices throughout the day and to control the size of my food portions.

I recognize that this contract is solely with myself and carries no rewards, penalties or punishments other than those associated with the reflection of the strength of my character.

Krista Clive-Smith

Wording the last paragraph to tie the commitment to my personal integrity all but guarantees I'll have deeply let myself down if I don't follow through, since my integrity is one of the things I value most. The key is that I don't *have to do it*. It's *a choice*. I could fall off the wagon and have no repercussions, and the world would keep on spinning. But I would know. By attaching my commitments to my own highest ideals I was able to help myself remain motivated at a cellular level to dig deeper and go after those things I know will take my life and legacy to the next level. And maybe, just maybe, if you're anything like me — perhaps this is helpful for you, too.

BODY / SELF IMAGE

British philosopher Ludwig Wittgenstein wrote, "The human body is the best picture of the human soul." If that's the case... *what does your body say about your inner self?*

If you're not happy with where you're at physically, or if your image of yourself is out of touch with reality, it affects you on levels you can't consciously imagine.

More than anything else, how you see yourself and how you feel about who you are from a body and self-image perspective dictates the inner makeup of your personal brand. I once saw a Budweiser beer ad showing a woman in a bikini with a caption that read, "Confidence. It's the sexiest thing you can wear." While I agree, sadly it's not something you can just go out and buy in a store.

Our self-image is formed by a combination of our past history and experiences, along with our emotions and feelings about ourselves. This is particularly interesting when you think about how much of our esteem can be related back to things that happen when we're kids.

As a child, you don't have the contextual framework to fully understand the meaning behind what people say. Various messages, if repeated, may lodge themselves into your tiny little brain and lay dormant. Just as a message will arrive at its destination wildly distorted if relayed verbally from person to person, such can be the case when the seed begins to sprout and you work to understand, years later, what happened in your childhood. We only have our recollection of how an event unfolded, which is at best our own perception. It may seem obvious as an adult that what someone said or did to us as a child wasn't done with the intention to psychologically scar us for life. In many cases, however, it did. And if it goes unnoticed, it may often repeat itself, continuing to destroy the self-image of the victim. This affects a person's level of confidence and self-esteem, which dramatically affects his or her personal brand.

Personally, I've been plagued with body image issues my whole life. I've always had a passion for food, but when competing in a sport like figure skating and then being thrust into the public eye when I won the local pageant title, I quickly developed a passion for people-pleasing and upholding a specific physical image as well.

My parents always told me I looked great. When I auditioned for an ice show and was told to lose ten pounds, my mom and dad told them they were crazy—I was healthy and beautiful just as I was. Knowing this, I've racked my brain over the years to figure out where on earth my issues originated.

Putting into words all of the different elements that comprise a personal brand has forced me to examine my own life in a new way. I've had a number of epiphanies and "aha" moments while writing this book. These moments of clarity have given me answers to the previously rhetorical question "why am I the way I am?" And this was one of them.

Imagine two kids standing side by side in front of you. They look very similar in build, yet when you go to lift them up, one is as light as a feather, and the other is what I call a 'tank'—it's as though this little person is made of lead.

From pictures of me as a child, one would assume I was as light as a feather. Wrong. I was a tank... no question about it. I wasn't very old when I came to realize this—it became quite obvious to me after having adults say "you're so heavy!" each time they picked me up, or when kids dropped me like a hot potato when piggybacking me for even a few steps.

At the time, I didn't know what "heavy," meant. It's a foreign concept to a child. I didn't begin to even think about my physical appearance until puberty. Then, all of a sudden

I started to notice myself gaining weight. It was kind of ironic, considering that when I hadn't paid any attention to it everything was fine, and the moment I realized I even had an appearance, it started to gang up on me.

I know now, with maturity, that when people used to say I was heavy, they didn't mean it in an overweight sense, just in a density context. But our society bases its judgment by the pound, and thus so did I. The internal belief that I was heavy became a self-fulfilling prophecy, and every day since about the age of thirteen I fought a battle with my weight. And until I finally worked through the issues that surrounded my body image, it had serious and negative consequences on both my confidence and self-esteem - and hence my personal brand.

You've heard me mention, even in my Ideal Day, that I work out. Believe me... it's got nothing to do with loving it. I don't. But I've realized that as much as I love food, nothing tastes as good as the way I feel when I'm on top of my game physically. Don't get me wrong: I'm not always consistent, and it doesn't mean I no longer indulge in my favorite foods. You know as well as I do what happens when people deny themselves certain foods. They might be good for awhile, but then a piece of cheesecake gets the best of them and suddenly it's got nothing to do with a chocolate bar here and there but an extra 20 lbs. of love around the equator.

> *Being strong and fit will make your day*
> *easier just like a good education will make*
> *your children's futures easier.*

DAVE PALADINO

The keys to balance are simple: everything in moderation

(including moderation), and pay attention to the math (input versus output). Exercise regularly, get your yearly medical check-ups, and do your best.

And as long as you're healthy, your weight in pounds has nothing to do with how you carry yourself in terms of your personal brand image. There are plenty of examples of this — even in Hollywood. Working in an industry where women have been traditionally very slight, there are more and more plus size models and actresses who are confident, sexy, and who carry their weight beautifully.

Regardless of what the scale says, to project an image of authentic confidence you need to come to terms with your natural body type and its relationship to your self-image. By learning to love yourself now, just as you are, you'll be dramatically changing your brand image from the inside out.

DISCIPLINE AND CHOICES

Discipline, to me, is training yourself to sacrifice what's easy to do and replacing it with what's right. It takes time, but as the days turn into weeks and months, all those small acts of daily commitment elevate your life to a new level. Daily discipline can produce extraordinary results that propel you closer to living the life you imagine.

Not only does discipline create a positive ripple effect in your outer world, its impact is even greater in your inner core. Few people realize how often they abuse the relationship they have with themselves. Yet they wonder why self-mastery is so difficult. If you repeatedly tell your closest friend you'll do something and then don't do it, there'll be an erosion of trust. The more often you break your promises, the less trust that person will have in you.

This is exactly what happens every time you make a deal with yourself but don't follow through. Your oldest and dearest friend is your inner self. You need to treat yourself with the same respect and unconditional love that you have for your other confidantes. Your relationship with yourself is the most important in your life, because it's inescapable. Hurt or betray those around you and you'll soon find they abandon you. Hurt or betray yourself, and you can't just leave the relationship.

Discipline is a choice, not a legacy.
To be disciplined or non-disciplined is a choice
you make every minute and every hour
of your life. It is something you do
and not something you have.

CHARLES J. GIVENS

Trust is the residue of promises kept. Having the courage to live up to your commitments — to others and to yourself — quickly spills into other areas of your life. By upholding even your smallest pledges, you build your capacity to follow through on larger promises. At the same time, you're strengthening the bond in the relationship you have with your inner self.

Discipline is, above all else, a choice. It's easy to see how a single choice can, in a heartbeat, cause us heartache for life and completely change the path we are on. If the name Monica Lewinsky rings a bell, no further explanation is needed to illustrate how your actions can forever alter your brand image in the marketplace!

You can have anything in life, but you can't have everything. You must make choices, and stand by them and love them as an extension of yourself. The greatest single power of a human being is the ability to choose. Sometimes this means you must rethink how you approach the opportunities that lie ahead. Self-mastery in life begins with self-mastery of your mind. Exercising your character one day at a time, little by little, shapes your will and strengthens your resolve. Above all else: keep your promises. Period. It will become one of the greatest defining brand attributes you could ever cultivate.

Idea Book Exercise

— Inner Self —

Write down the answers to the following questions in your
Idea Book.

Discipline and Choices   DATE: _____

What one thing, if you did it today, would propel you
further toward the achievement of your goals?

What changes, if any, need to be made so that your
vision of a healthy future can become a reality?

What one act of daily discipline will you practice
for the next 21 days?

....

....

....

....

....

....

....

....

....

....

....

Exploring Your

OUTER
SELF

*Fashion is not simply a matter
of clothes. Fashion is in the air, born
upon the wind. One intuits it.
It is in the sky and on
the road.*

GABRIELLE "COCO" CHANEL

FOUR AREAS OF YOUR LIFE contribute to the creation of your
external personal brand:

PHYSICAL APPEARANCE

PERSONAL STYLE

WARDROBE

YOUR OUTER SANCTUMS:
Transportation, Home, Office

Physical appearance

Dramatic increases in cosmetic surgery suggest our society is obsessed with physical appearance. Many people feel the need to change certain aspects of their exterior look. While I'm not an advocate for cosmetically changing your body, I accept that in some cases a perceived deficiency in a physical feature can hamper someone's own self-image to the extent that they're unable to be confident and happy. A great example is teeth: if you're self-conscious about your teeth and as a result you rarely smile, a couple of thousand dollars may be a wise lifetime investment.

In this section, you'll find examples of people in the public eye who have utilized a trait, feature, or their personal style to define their individualism in the marketplace. As you go through each element, think about how it could be utilized as a key component in the packaging and development of your own personal brand and signature style.

Physical Features

A caricaturist can create a likeness of you in mere minutes, simply by exaggerating your most distinct physical characteristics. In essence, that's what we're doing with personal branding—packaging your identity into a set of distinguishable features that make you instantly recognizable.

Your physical features are a great place to begin looking for traits that make you unique. Think of Barbara Streisand: she most certainly could have changed the appearance of her nose, but thankfully she didn't. Her nose became an outstanding feature and helped her stand out in a sea of actors and musicians. She's recognized for it, yet it plays no role in the actual content of her brand promise or her abilities as an entertainer.

Sometimes it's not one particular feature that makes a person recognizable, but rather, how he or she uses it. In the case of Jim Carrey, it's the way he contorts his face and body. With Morgan Freeman, James Earl Jones, Alan Rickman (Harry Potter's Snape), and Clint Eastwood, it's the way they utilized their voices to portray particular characters.

Other examples of people who have utilized a unique physical feature as a brand identifier include Mick Jagger (lips), Jennifer Lopez and Kim Kardashian (butts), Prince Charles (ears), Dolly Parton (breasts), Frank Sinatra (eye color), Arnold Schwarzenegger (muscles), and Betty Grable, whose "million dollar legs"were, in fact, insured for that very amount!

Think about your own physical features and which ones represent you best. The exercise on the following page will help you determine which of your physical attributes are best suited to becoming a target feature in your own brand image.

Idea Book Exercise

— Outer Self —

Write down the answers to the following questions in your
Idea Book.

Physical Appearance   DATE: _____

Which facial features and body parts are most
identifiably your own? If unsure, ask a friend or imagine
how a caricaturist might draw a sketch of your
likeness.

How can you utilize what's unique about your looks
and make the most of these traits in the development
of your own personal brand?

YOUR PERSONAL STYLE

Hairstyle

Your hairstyle can go a long way to identifying you as a unique individual; it's one of the cornerstones of your personal brand. The styling products you use, along with the length, style, and color of your hair contribute dramatically to your overall look. You can easily manipulate the perception of your entire brand promise based on this one feature alone.

Tennis player Andre Agassi utilized his hairstyle for more than just looks. When he burst onto the world tennis scene, everything about him was wild and unconventional. His long hair immediately separated him from his competitors, and the increased media attention because of that gave him a heightened profile. His revolutionary hairdo was consistent with his values and belief system — he continued to be a non-conformist when he became the first player to wear anything but white at Wimbledon. Later in his career, when he was in the comeback stage, his hairstyle reflected a new-found maturity and priorities: now a family man, his long locks were gone. Instead, he shaved his head and opted for a simple, more conservative look.

Even fictional characters' hairstyles can (and do) reflect their personal brands. By changing the style, color and/or length of a character's hair, a dramatic new look can symbolize a new stage in his or her evolution. Think of Elsa's transformation in Frozen, or even Clark Kent versus Superman. And in the case of someone like Madonna who's continually finding ways to reinvent herself and changes her hairstyle frequently, her *consistent pattern of inconsistency* has become a hallmark of her personal brand.

Your hair not only affects your personal brand from the outside, but can have a dramatic effect on your self-image and inner brand as well. As a young figure skater, I idolized the likes of Dorothy Hamill and Jill Trenary, both short-haired women who oozed personality and charm. Trying to be like them, I wore my hair short for most of my adolescent life. Between the ages of eight and twelve I was mistaken for a boy on a number of occasions, which absolutely crushed me (and certainly explains why I wore such huge earrings as a teenager—no one was EVER going to mistake me for a boy again!). I toughed it out and kept my short hair until I won the local pageant title when I was 17.

By that time I had begun to come into my own in the looks department, but even with a crown upon my head, something wasn't right: I still didn't feel beautiful, or feminine-looking. I know now it was just the residue left over from comments made by complete strangers in my youth, but those comments had become a part of my internal belief system.

Something as simple as my hairstyle had drastically affected my self-image for almost a decade, and it had to end. As my hair grew longer, my feelings about myself began to change, giving me a new confidence about my sexuality and femininity. Of course, this new-found confidence radiated from within, completely changing my external brand image as well as my internal one.

There are so many women in the world that look fabulous with short hair, and their confidence and esteem is made stronger as a result. As with everything it's a personal choice. Much more important than how you look on the outside is how you feel on the inside. Whatever you choose, pick a hairstyle that makes you walk a little taller, and smile a little more brightly.

Other examples of high-profile personalities whose hairstyle (or lack thereof) is a defining feature of their personal brand include Donald Trump, Albert Einstein and even Star Wars' Princess Leia.

Facial Hair

Terry Bollea, better known as wrestling superstar Hulk Hogan, has used his trademark white-blonde hair and handlebar mustache to portray more than one personality in the ring. Hulk Hogan went from good guy to bad guy with the introduction of Hollywood Hogan, but he was able to maintain consistency of character—one person with two very different temperaments—simply by growing out the facial hair along his jawline between his mustache and sideburns and coloring that portion of his beard black. The rest was the same, yet this one slight alteration trans-formed him from a positive, upbeat personality into a dark, mean, bad guy character.

> *I refuse to think of them as chin hairs. I think of them as stray eyebrows.*
>
> JANETTE BARBER

Many other people in the public eye are known for their facial hair—the famous eyebrows of Frida Kahlo; Elvis Presley's distinctive sideburns; the eyebrow/mustache combo of Groucho Marx and Charlie Chaplin; the well-known mustache of Adolph Hitler; the familiar beards of Jesus Christ, Abraham Lincoln, and Santa Claus.

Jewelry

Many feel that "less is best" when it comes to jewelry, yet

the use of different signature pieces or gemstones, or even the amount of jewelry that you wear, can become a brand trademark in itself.

On both men and women, jewelry can be anything from a small indicator to a dead giveaway of personality, status, lifestyle and attitude. Your watch can tell a lot about the type of person you are. If you wear a timepiece with a stop-watch feature and a synthetic wristband, for example, most people will assume that you're a sporty, adventurous or outdoorsy type of person; a Rolex indicates wealth. The quantity and quality of your jewelry speaks volumes about you as an individual. An excessive personality through and through, Elizabeth Taylor even wrote a book entitled *Elizabeth Taylor: My Love Affair with Jewelry*. She is perhaps the greatest example of someone whose brand identity is inextricably linked to jewelry. It's not just women: men and the jewelry they wear can become an outstanding feature of their personal brands.

Oprah is quite the opposite. One of the wealthiest women in the world makes a very large statement by not wearing much jewelry even though she can afford to. In addition, her short, well-groomed, natural-looking nails showcase her unpretentious nature and core value set. The combination of very little jewelry and a low-maintenance approach to grooming evokes a trust that few people with such celebrity status have ever successfully achieved with the public en mass. We feel as though she's one of us, even though most definitely she is a part of another world living a lifestyle most of us can only dream about. Neither approach is right or wrong. They are just two different styles creating vastly different perceptions. By looking at examples from both sides of the coin, perhaps you'll be able to find a style that speaks to you and feels like a good fit for your own personal brand.

Piercings and Tattoos

Whether you have one small initial hidden from view or you've covered a large portion of your skin with body art, tattoos are a more permanent depiction of what you stand for. Most people choose the design after careful consideration, and rightly so, for tattoos are a defining brand attribute. Tattoos are intensely personal, heavy in symbolism and representative of events, relationships, milestones or beliefs. Similar to jewelry and accessories, your choice of tattoos and piercings allow you to wear your heart on your sleeve — literally!

Makeup & Perfume/Cologne

Subtle or bold, makeup can define your features and highlight your face, often dramatically changing the way you look. And it's not just for women, either. Whether it's a full face of makeup like Michael Jackson, a slick of black nail polish on one fingernail like Ozzy Osbourne, or just a touch up for TV cameras, it's becoming more and more accepted — and popular — for men to wear makeup, even on an everyday basis.

> *The real aim of makeup is not*
> *to adorn but to beautify.*
>
> COCO CHANEL

Coco Chanel may be right, but obviously not everyone subscribes to her advice! Three words exemplify that fact: Tammy Faye Baker. Her multiple layers of mascara became a brand trademark for her personal image. You can consistently utilize one type of makeup as singer Adele also does with liquid eyeliner, or you can build a reputation with a particular shade as Gwen Stefani has done with scarlet lipstick. Another option is to cover your face entirely in a cosmetic mask like members of the band KISS.

Nails and nail polish reveal more about a person than how much they use their hands. They provide clues to personality type and attention to detail. One can assume different things by noting such things as length, whether the nails are chewed or filed, color of nail polish, whether they are natural or faux nails, and the overall condition of a person's nails and cuticles. Olympic runner Florence Griffith Joyner, known to her fans simply as Flo-Jo, captivated the world with her phenomenal speed and a flamboyant personal style that included trademark six-inch painted fingernails.

Another powerful way to be remembered is through your choice (and quantity) of fragrance. Both help others discern your personality and provides them with clues about your lifestyle and interests. Your scent creates a lasting memory of you in the minds of the people who surround you. Pleasurable or offensive, it's easy for a certain smell to become associated with your personal brand. It can prolong the recollection of you in people's minds when they catch a waft of the same (or similar) scent, even years later. Just as certain songs have the power to "take you back," smells can also act as a catalyst to trigger memories. There's an entire industry known as "Scent Marketing" which focuses on infusing retail and other spaces with signature fragrances for exactly this purpose. Whether you choose to wear one signature scent, or to frequently change your perfume or cologne to reflect your mood, be aware that you may be making your entrance even before you physically walk into a room!

Accessories

Success often consists of doing small things right. I believe this to be true in paying attention to your use of accessories as well, beyond those we discussed above. Some examples are your choice of:

- Eyeglasses (style of frame, choice to wear glasses versus contacts, etc.)
- Sunglasses
- Handbag, wallet and/or briefcase
- Hat
- Business card holder
- Keychain
- Paper-based planner vs. electronic
- Cell phone
- The type of pen you carry (or don't!)
- Lifestyle-related props

Other men and women who have highlighted their personal brands through the use of accessories and accent pieces include: Woody Allen and John Lennon (glasses), Michael Jackson (single glove), Larry King (glasses and suspenders), Nelly (Band-Aid), George Burns (cigar), Bono (blue sunglasses), Charlie Chaplin (Bowler hat and cane), Paris Hilton (dog carrier handbag/purse).

YOUR WARDROBE

Clothes define you. That's a given. But it's not about wearing big-name brands or labels. It's about finding a style that suits your personality and body type. You want to look and feel great—as well as to communicate your personal brand to the outside world. Personal style transcends high fashion every time!

Imagine opening your closet door, putting on the first thing you see and walking out your door looking fabulous, every time.

If you buy clothes like most people do, it's next to impossible. You know—a pair of pants here, a great top there, the latest trend must-have, the odd I-can't-live-without-it outfit and my own personal favorite—"but it was on sale!"

> *My closet is full, but*
> *I've got nothing to wear!*
>
> MY CLIENTS

When you shop on an item-by-item basis, randomly choosing pieces individually, it's no wonder you feel you have nothing to wear. It's like picking up capers, ice cream and thyme at the grocery store and wondering why you can't make a meal. An item of clothing may very well be on sale, and a good deal, but it doesn't mean you should buy it. The key is to think about how much you're spending (not just saving), and to ask yourself this all-important question: "If it wasn't on sale and I had to pay not just full retail, but a *premium* for it, would I be as excited about buying this right now?" If the answer is no, fight every urge and buying impulse in your body and put it back.

The 80/20 rule seems to apply in almost any situation, and it certainly holds true in fashion. If you were to pull out all the items in your closet and separate them into two piles, frequent versus occasional wear, chances are you'll find you wear only 20 per cent of your wardrobe 80 per cent of the time. Your favorites. We all have them. The key is to expand your favorites to form a base "uniform," and then develop your own signature style by investing in trend-forward, stylish accent pieces. Just as in art, the core of your closet is a blank canvas, a simple yet versatile backdrop on which to express your individualism and personality, your true inner essence.

When you think about celebrities and their differing personal styles, consider the motivation behind the clothes they wear. Many famous men and women hire clothing stylists, people whose sole occupation is to ensure that they dress in a way that supports and perpetuates the public image they've cultivated. If you've ever watched the Academy Awards, you'll know that what the stars are wearing is every bit as important as who walks away with the golden hardware at the end of the night. Even if you haven't ever seen the annual awards show on TV, chances are good you've seen photos or heard people talking the next day about "who wore what" as they walked the red carpet.

The term "fashion statement" sums it up well. The clothes you wear act as a public advertisement for your personality. Whether you choose to make a bold or a subtle statement is entirely up to you, but be aware that even if you attempt to *not* make any statement at all, verbally or otherwise, your wardrobe will do so on your behalf.

One year, at the MTV Video Music Awards, Lady Gaga wore a dress made from raw beef (a.k.a. the "meat dress"), as a means of making a silent statement about one's need to fight for what they believe in. She later explained her interpretation of the dress to Ellen DeGeneres, stating, "If we don't stand up for what we believe in and if we don't stand up for our rights, pretty soon we're going to have as much rights as the meat on our bones."

Learning how to dress well is not as difficult as it may seem. Like golf, it is an acquired skill that can be honed and improved with correct practice.

ALAN FLUSSER

Women such as Jacqueline Kennedy Onassis, Princess Diana and Audrey Hepburn took a completely different - and more conservative - approach with the fashion statements they made. They were considered fashion icons, wearing clothes that were fashion-forward and trendy, yet had staying power that has ended up lasting decades. Their classically beautiful styles have transcended generations and still remain as elegant and appropriate today as they were years ago.

Whether it's in the boardroom or on the street, everyday men and women get noticed for, and are remembered by the clothes they wear. Steve Jobs made a black shirt and jeans his uniform of choice. Even golfer Tiger Woods utilizes symbolism to promote his brand image—not only does he wear his sponsor's logo on his clothing, but he's made the clothes themselves symbolic by regularly wearing a red golf shirt on the final day (Sunday) of a tournament.

Now that you've explored what other people have done to reflect their inner selves through the clothes they wear, it's time to develop your own wardrobe strategy to externally package your authentic personal brand.

Idea Book Exercise

— Outer Self —

This ten-step plan will help you build a wardrobe that defines and appropriately displays your personal style.

Ten Step Plan For Wardrobe Development

1. Pull out your Personal Style folder from the set of three 'Style Files' you've assembled. Look at the photos. Can you distinguish any patterns between the fashion styles or different looks you were drawn to? Are most of the models wearing suits or more casual clothing? Is there any similarity in the style, whether in the length, rise, etc.? For women, were the models in skirts more often than pants, or vice versa? Do you notice any common denominators in terms of accessories, jewelry, etc.? Try to determine why you chose each photo, and what part of it appeals to you. The more commonalities you can find, the closer you'll be to finding the pattern behind your 'base uniform' that will make you feel your best.

2. Answer these questions in your Idea Book:

   · What is my basic body type or shape?

      – Triangle (bottom heavy)

      – Inverted Triangle (top heavy)

      – Rectangle (undefined waist—similar chest, waist and hip measurements)

      – Circle (round overall, with a full midsection)

- What colors look best on me? If you don't know, try holding up different pieces of fabric or items of clothing under your chin and you'll start to see right away which shades look better with your skin coloring.

- What is my personal fashion style?

  - Classic: tailored, sophisticated

  - Fashion-forward: trendy, what's hot

  - Dramatic: creative, bold

  - Casual: comfortable, easy

  - Alternative: grunge, edgy

  - Vintage: subtle patterns, aged-looking

- What type of clothing does my lifestyle warrant? Attach a percentage beside each category, to add up to one hundred per cent (your total wardrobe):

  - Formal

  - Business

  - Business casual

  - Casual

  - Workout

3. Now it's time to get down and dirty: time to clean out your closet! The first stage is preparation: get three boxes and label them Keep, Donate/Give Away, and Fix. You'll also need a trash can and a shopping bag for a very small pile of 'special' items to be discussed in Step 7.

4. Eliminate everything that doesn't fit or that you haven't worn in a year. Period. That includes getting rid of all of your "skinny clothes," too! Hanging on to clothes that no

longer fit erodes your self-esteem by sending a subconscious message to your brain that it's not all right to be just the way you are. If you're convinced they're a motivational tool for weight loss, why not decide up-front to reward your successes with new, up-to-date clothes that show off your weight-loss accomplishments instead?

5. Look at each piece of clothing in your closet, on an item by item basis, through the eyes of a fashion detective. As you look at each piece, ask yourself:

   · Does it fit me properly?

   · Is it flattering to my body type?

   · Does it make me feel great every time I put it on?

   · What does it say about me?

   · Does it represent who I am and who I want to be?

   · Does this item define and express the essence
     of my personality?'

   · Does it need any alterations... stain removal,
     buttons sewed on, etc.?

   Answering these questions will make it easier to decide which clothes go in which box. Still not sure? Try on each item and give it a mark out of ten. Once you've given each item a grade, eliminate the lowest-scoring ones.

6. Keep a running list of any items you'll need to replace (for example, if you throw out your only bathing suit, put 'new bathing suit' on the list). Add only the things you really must replace, or that you will need to acquire that you don't already own.

7. Put any items that are simply too hard to part with—for financial or sentimental reasons—or those that are practically new but not quite right into the shopping bag. Share them with a friend with the caveat that if you really, really want them back some day, they can loan (but not give) them back to you!

8. Next, set pride aside. Invite one of your closest friends over, one whose sense of style you admire. Using a digital camera, go through the clothes that survived the first seven steps and, outfit by outfit, model different combinations for the lens. Strange? Of course it is. But how many times have you gone out thinking that you looked just fine in something, only to see a photo later and wonder what the heck you were thinking (or realize it perhaps was not as flattering on you as you thought it was)?

9. When your closet has been thinned out and you feel great about how every single item of clothing looks on you and makes you feel, take a step back and view your wardrobe as a whole, looking for color trends and style patterns. It may be helpful to put like-items together and separate your closet into a section for each (casual versus dress shirts, pants, jackets, sweaters, etc.).

10. Deliver the Donate/Give Away box and the shopping bag to their new homes, empty the trash can, and relax. The hard part is over. You've already got the skeleton of your basic look, as well as some favorite pieces. Your last step is to fill in the gaps. Time to go SHOPPING!

YOUR OUTER SANCTUMS:
TRANSPORTATION, HOME, OFFICE

Transportation

In addition to sizing you up by your clothes, people form impressions based on your choice of vehicle (or your method of transportation). As with clothing, cost is not the only factor. Style plays a larger role.

Visualize each of the following types of automobiles. What image comes to mind about the person (or the stereotype of that person) behind the wheel?

Minivan

Sports car

Classic or collector car

Pickup truck

Motorcycle

Four-door sedan

Sport utility vehicle

Off-road vehicle

Convertible

Now look at how different models can affect a person's image, using convertibles as the example. All the cars on the next list are 'topless,' but each make and model conveys a different message and evokes a different emotional response. What image of the stereotypical driver of each model of car comes to mind, and what personality attributes would you suggest might go along with each stereotype?

Porsche Boxster

Volkswagen Beetle

Ford Thunderbird Classic

Chrysler Sebring

Jeep Wrangler

Rolls-Royce Corniche

Ford Mustang

Vastly different, aren't they?

Just as you were able to come up with suggestions for the personality types of the drivers above, people are able to come up with suggestions about your personality type by assessing your vehicle or method of transportation. You don't need to drive a new or fancy automobile in order for your brand to be complimented—the upkeep, cleanliness and personal touches you add are more than capable of leaving a great impression, regardless of what type of vehicle you own.

In the same way that logos and messages on your t-shirt express your inner self, the accessories you add to your vehicle make a statement about your personality. Some examples are:

Personalized license plates

Vehicle decals (ie. corporate logos, racing stripes)

Bumper stickers

Rearview mirror accessories (ie. dice)

Tinted windows

Ground effects, spoilers, fins

(Oversize) tires, and rims

Roof racks, carrying cases, etc.

Upholstery vs. leather interior

Stereo/Entertainment system

Wifi

Imagine you're sitting in a job interview for a sales position with a major corporation, and having a vehicle is required for the job. As the meeting ends, the person interviewing you stands up and says,"Thanks so much for coming in! Would you mind if I caught a ride up the street with you? It's just a few blocks, and my car is at the mechanic today." What is your immediate emotional reaction about having the interviewer see the inside of your car?

You never know who will ask you for a ride or need to look inside your trunk. Be prepared, and whether clean or messy - by choice - make sure that your desired brand image is appropriately reflected in the state of your vehicle.

Home

An invitation into someone's home is an invitation into their private, inner world. Think about the following factors and how they contribute to the opinions you've formed about others, based on their living quarters:

Location

Décor

Setup and/or layout

Possessions

The sensory experience (smells, sounds, visual appeal, the feel of the home, the taste of food or beverages)

Similarly, your own physical environment heavily influences other people's impressions of you and your brand. Your home reveals clues about your financial status, relationships, culture, religion, hobbies, employment and education. It tells others about your personality, thoughts, beliefs and ideals. To an onlooker, your home and its contents are a three-dimensional, living collection of your past and present life.

> *Like it or not, the personalities of our homes*
> *are accurate barometers that reflect where we*
> *have been, what's going on in our lives,*
> *and who we are today, though not*
> *necessarily where we're heading.*

SARAH BAN BREATHNACH

The goal of this detective game is to inspire you to look closely at where and how you live. The intention is to bring you one step closer to feeling as though you're fully integrated as a human being—with your inner and outer selves perfectly aligned, living your most authentic life.

Your living space should be a sanctum that embraces you physically and emotionally every time you're in it. Moreover, it should include a space your can call your own —a refuge from the chaos, a place to just be. By creating an environment that speaks to you, you'll have a nourishing haven for mind and soul—a place where you can read, write, think, or just exist.

Consider what it would be like to have a corner, or even an entire room, filled only with things you love. When you walk into this space the walls embrace you in a hug perfectly contoured to your every facet—the way water completely surrounds your entire being when you're swimming. Nurturing and supporting your highest ideals, your private haven embodies the true meaning of the word "home."

When I do one-on-one personal brand and organizing consulting, a portion of time is dedicated to helping clients create such a space. Many clients feel creating this inner sanctum ignites a ripple effect throughout the other facets of their life.

One client, a songwriter and actress, chose to transform her home studio. Her husband felt so passionate about the change it made in her life that he wrote me the following letter, sharing his third-party perspective on the results:

"My wife has always used the spare bedroom in our house as the nerve centre for all of her activities. She does her work-related phoning and e-mailing from there, but also uses the room for vocal practice, songwriting, and other creative pursuits.

As an unused bedroom, the space had never been utilized in a thought-out manner, let alone decorated, apart from a few pictures with nowhere else to go. The room eventually collected quite a hodge-podge assortment of musical instruments, old audio equipment, books and tapes, etc., in the midst of which sat her desk and piano.

On the whole, the room seemed to be quite functional, and I don't recall her ever complaining about its layout or appearance. She just went up there every day, tea in hand, and went about her work. The only indication that the room might not be living up to its potential was the fact that she often said she did her best songwriting away from the house.

You helped her to see for herself how her work-space was out of sync with her own ideas of what made for a comfortable, enjoyable environment with the startling observations about how various aspects of the room's contents, layout and appear-ance were actually hampering her ability to do her best work there.

Taken individually, the changes the room under-went were far from major. A lot of unused 'junk' was taken out, and the room got a coat of paint in my wife's favorite color. The existing furniture was aug-mented with a cast-off daybed from her mother's house. A few of her most cherished accessories from around the house made their way into the room: her lava lamp, some candles, and a couple of her favorite coffee-table books. Not a lot of time or money seemed to have to go into the project.

The whole, however, has been far greater than the sum of its parts. The revamped room is almost unrec-ognizable, despite containing most of its original furniture. There is an immediate impression of beauty, comfort, and rightness the moment you walk in the door. From the piano bench, there is now an uplifting view through the branches of a towering elm tree to the quiet street beyond. Away from the wall, the old mahogany desk is now remarkably inviting. The new/old daybed's presence seems to suggest that working in this room is completely optional.

Guess again! Since the makeover, my wife has been able to rattle off her daily communications with unprecedented comfort and ease. What's more, she's finally able to relax enough in her workspace for the songwriting ideas to flow as easily at home as they do in far-flung places. The most unexpected change is that the room is now so open and inviting that she is now able to have people over for rehearsals, meetings and writing sessions, things that used to be scheduled for whatever makeshift outside space could be found. It would be an understatement to say that she now enjoys her work more than ever. Formerly relegated to an "unused" room, my wife's projects now come to light in a space especially designed for the purpose. The difference in the relationship she has with her work is remarkable. There seems to be an element of joy surrounding tasks that were more like obligations before. And you've never seen someone make it up a flight of stairs with a mug of tea so quickly!"

Even if your house isn't perfect for you, a few minor alterations can make it a warm and inviting home that reflects your true authentic self. The best way to transform your current dwelling into a remarkable residence is to heed the sage advice of William Morris, a 19th century English designer who said,"Have nothing in your houses that you do not know to be useful or believe to be beautiful." Simplify, and utilize the ideas you've culled from the photos and articles in your Style File folders or Pinterest boards labeled "Home." The result will be a safe and sacred space from which you can truly be your most authentic self - inside and out.

Idea Book Exercise

— Outer Self —

Start a few pages in your Idea Book dedicated to your ideal domicile (I have four pages called My Dream Home; I left two of them blank, so that I can add ideas after visiting a friend's house or walking through a show home). The purpose of the Dream Home list is to describe in detail all the nooks, crannies and features of your ultimate living space—the one you'll build or buy one day!

My Dream Home   DATE: _____

ACTION ITEM: Now that you've formulated your thoughts into notes on this page, transfer your ideas for your Dream Home into your Idea Book. Remember to leave space at the end so you add new things as you think of them.

YOUR OFFICE

Wouldn't Monday mornings feel a little less onerous if your office was a nurturing environment reminiscent of your home?

Decorating your workspace with a personal touch can make it seem more like a home away from home. Just as the clothes you wear to work project a certain image, your office reflects many facets of your personality to the outside world. Your internal and external customers (company staff and clients) can tell a lot about your goals, achievements, hobbies and life by looking around the surface area of your office.

Keeping in mind the corporate brand image of your company, your goal is to maintain just the right balance of personality and professionalism in your office décor. Don't go so hog wild that you lose sight of its purpose: your office is still the place in which the work of a business is done. The key is moderation: the last thing you want is for your office to be mistaken as a retail hobby store, unless, of course, that's what it is!

The most important elements in your office are the chairs. In this one area, always sacrifice style for comfort. If you sit at your desk all day, make sure your office chair is adjustable and ergonomically suited to your body. And, don't forget the chairs opposite your desk if you have them. If this is the place where clients regularly make their purchasing decisions, ensure that the chairs you offer them are extremely comfortable. It's a subtle detail, yet it's the core of your business. The same holds true for any company: focus on the "little things" at the physical point where the buying decision is usually made.

Decorate your workspace to reflect your personal interests, and showcase your individualism through a mix of business and pleasure. The following list of accessories will give you some points of inspiration on ways to inject some personality into your office décor:

- Area rug(s)
- Artwork, photographs, mirrors, calendars, posters, and other wall hangings & frames
- Books & reading material
- Business card holder, pens, letter openers, paperweights
- Clocks
- Souvenirs/travel memorabilia
- Collectibles
- Diplomas/certificates, plaques, trophies and awards
- Furniture & lamps
- Knick-knacks
- Memorabilia
- Plants
- Telephone(s)
- Time management/organization items or storage containers
- Coffee mug or water glass

By making your office a reflection of your inner self, you invite the people you do business with to get to know you a little better. Creating that emotional connection not only fosters a new level of trust with your clients, it also eliminates some of the heavy lifting in the sales process by making it an enjoyable experience for the customer as well.

CHAMPIONING
Your Brand

Choosing who to invite into the inner sanctum of your home

You Are Hereby

GUILTY BY ASSOCIATION

Your human environment: the lovers, friends and colleagues you choose to include in your life, contribute to the impression of who you are, or who you want to be.

JO-ELLAN DIMITRIUS & MARK MAZZARELLA

As IF DEFINING, POSITIONING AND PACKAGING your personal brand isn't enough! To effectively round out your strategy you must look closely at the people who are, or may become, associated with your brand. This list will include:

BUSINESS RELATIONSHIPS:
Customers, Clients, Employees, Co-workers

PERSONAL NETWORK:
Friends, Acquaintances

FAMILY MEMBERS

SPOUSE / LIFE PARTNER

MENTORS

You're judged by association, whether you like it or not. The key is to manage your relationships and understand with whom your brand will be linked. It's important to surround yourself with a team that that makes up for your weaknesses and strengthens your brand. Equally important is surrounding yourself with a team that inspires you and that you love to be around. This team includes your business relationships, life partner/spouse, friends, and acquaintances. Let's look more closely at each of these groups.

BUSINESS RELATIONSHIPS:
Customers, Clients, Employees, Co-workers

Earlier we discussed the importance of gearing your business to deal primarily with your ideal clients and customers—those clients who give you the most job satisfaction and joy, as well as profitability and return on investment.

This makes sense for another reason: credibility. Having clients on your list who are consistent with the market you want to attract, and having positive testimonials from those clients, builds trust and brand integrity. When you can say you have a business relationship with so and so, and they're willing to attach their name and/or image to your brand, you garner word-of-mouth buzz and a heightened profile. For this reason, many companies use prominent sports or entertainment figures as spokespeople for their products or services. Having a mega-star promoting your brand would be nice, but for most people and many companies it's not that realistic. If you've positioned yourself correctly, however, you'll already have a portfolio of many reputable clients actively promoting your brand. Their collective voices and far-reaching networks will bring in far more qualified leads and substantial new business opportunities than a misaligned or unrelated big name ever could.

> *Never do business with people you*
> *don't trust. Life's too short.*
>
> HARRY QUADRACCI

Not only do your clients form perceptions by brand association, they also form them based on your internal customers (employees, management team and ownership group). You're subconsciously being evaluated on the conduct, appearance and actions of the people you work with, and by those you hire. When you're a part of a company, you're often judged as a package deal. Recruiting, then, is particularly important, and so it should be. Who you bring into the business to represent you may be the single most important corporate decision you ever make. Management guru Tom Peters says it best in his book, *The Pursuit of WOW*:

> "Your recruiting process should say to the candidate, 'How'd you like to be part of our community, do neat things together, grow individually and with your peers?' Hence recruiting becomes a painstaking, two-way courting ritual, complete with coffee dates, flirting, weekend strolls, dinner with the parents, proposals on bended knee, and an

exchange of solemn vows of fidelity. Is my recruiting model expensive? Yep. But what's more important than recruiting?"

Your internal and external customers are your brand champions — the people who carry your brand out into the marketplace. They are in essence your brand's spokespeople, and they represent your brand by association. Making sure they fit the part is an important part of your personal brand strategy.

PERSONAL NETWORK:
Friends, Acquaintances

I agree with the statement, "It's not what you know, it's who you know," but only to a point. I think another line should be added that reads "even more important than who you know, is who knows *you*."

Have no friends not equal to yourself.

CONFUCIUS

I once heard someone say if you want to see the future of your net worth, take a look around and the average net worth of the five people you spend the most time with is where your own is headed. While that might be true financially, it's definitely true when it comes to the impact of personal associations on your brand. Thomas Bailey Aldrich summed it up perfectly when he said, "A man is known by the company his mind keeps."

The people you choose to share your life with speak volumes about who you are and the qualities you hold near and dear. They also serve an important role in the internal development of your personal brand. Think of the space in your heart that's reserved for personal relationships as a cup. Those friends who accept you and love you fill up that cup; those who are constantly judging or criticizing you deplete it. Is your cup half empty? Half full? Does your cup runneth over?

Idea Book Exercise

— Guilty By Association—

Make a list of names in your circle of influence (people meaningful to you by virtue of the time you spend with them or in the quality of their place in your life).

My Circle of Influence   DATE: _____

Go back over your list and put an N beside those who Nurture you and a T beside those who are Toxic. Your challenge is to eliminate the Ts from your life in the coming year. You might think it's not as easy as it sounds, but you won't know until you try, and the results may very well surprise you. They certainly surprised me! I woke up one day with the realization that life is too short to maintain a façade of friendship with people who don't (and won't ever) accept me as I am, flaws and all. It's just too much work with no return on investment. I didn't read anyone the riot act, nor did I inform the offenders that I was eliminating them from my life. I just quit calling. Period. I didn't burn any bridges— I merely quit trying to repair them. A funny thing happened when I stopped calling—I began to realize that they weren't calling me, either! Slowly, my world changed. Ruled by love in all senses of the word, I became more confident, and my insecurities began to vanish, one by one. I began celebrating my weaknesses rather than beating myself up over them. Externally, these changes were apparent to everyone around me.

Think of the Ts you've listed above that you're aiming to eliminate. As you get closer to living the life you love, many of them will help out this process by beginning to distance themselves from you naturally. Misery loves company, and as you grow and achieve and succeed, you'll be less likely to be good company for the Ts in your life. Don't worry, though: success also feeds off itself. You'll begin to meet new people on your path - other fantastic individuals equally committed to living the life they were meant to live. I'm sure you'll find, like I did, that for every T you eliminate, you'll gain at least two (or more) new Ns. Your friends and acquaintances affect others' perceptions of you and your personal brand. More importantly, they affect who you are as a human being. Choose them carefully. Just as you cleaned out your closet, take a stand, and eliminate those people that are no longer a fit. Surround yourself with the nurturing support system you deserve. Your life will never be the same.

FAMILY MEMBERS

You might be wondering why I didn't ask you to include family members in the circle of influence exercise. The reason is simple: you didn't get to choose them. They were given to you, or you to them. Family members are put in a different category than those with whom you've made the conscious decision to include in your life, even though the end result may be the same. If some, or even all, members of your family are toxic influences, perhaps you need to re-evaluate their involvement in your life. You might want to seek counseling, or to invite a group discussion to bring your feelings out into the open.

Regardless of how you do it, by articulating your limits you've taken back your power. Often the toxic relationships in our lives have an emotional stranglehold over us, and voicing your boundaries will loosen the grip.

There is a vast difference between establishing boundaries and putting up emotional walls, however. Please don't confuse the two. Boundaries are invisible lines you draw between what you will and won't stand for. For boundaries to be effective, they must be clearly communicated. Walls are barriers to open communication — they can be climbed, and they can be torn down, but while they're standing there can be little or no interaction. Sure, you can hide behind the walls you've built, but not only do they keep out the bad guys — they also prevent the good ones from coming in.

Whether you choose to keep toxic influences in your daily life or decide to let them be, your decision defines your brand — and your life — on a more macro level. As long as you're in the driver's seat, proactively making decisions rather than responding, reacting, or having someone else make choices for you, you'll be fine. The key is to *select*, don't settle!

SPOUSE / LIFE PARTNER

It's been said that who we marry accounts for ninety per cent of our happiness. While I would've preferred to hear that we account for ninety per cent of our own happiness, it certainly raises an interesting point. Who you choose to spend your life with has an enormous impact on your life's happiness and your personal brand.

According to millionaires surveyed in the book *The Millionaire Mind,* the top five qualities contributing to successful marriages are:

> Honesty
> Responsibility
> Loving
> Capable
> Supportive

Honesty tops the list for many, yet in the courtship phase of a relationship, the vast majority of people censor parts of their authentic self. They fear that revealing past history or exposing a particular personality trait will turn the other person away. Our humanness has become something we initially shy away from in relationships. Maybe singer Macy Gray was on to something when she said, "I'm really demanding. No girl wants just a guy. You want a prince, you want Jesus. So when he comes around and his name is, like, Steve, what are you supposed to do?"

A part of us is always searching for perfection, but in relationships, I think we have misconstrued what perfect means. It's not about being perfect, because the nature of humanity is that we're blessed with both strengths and weaknesses, and our different characteristics appeal to some but offend others. The perfection that we search for is more aptly defined as being perfect *for one another*.

Censoring any part of your personality changes the natural fit between you and your partner, and vice versa. You can't expect your partner to stretch out, loosen up, calm down or change in any way. You need to expect that what you sign up for is what you get, flaws and all, for the duration of your relationship.

Your spouse or life partner reflects a facet of your personal brand to the outside world, but your love relationship has the greatest impact on your brand on the inside. Relationships, especially the romantic variety, cause you to think and even conduct yourself differently than you might otherwise. They have a magical way of tinting your view of the world — coloring your perceptions, actions and feelings. The dynamics of your partnership shapes your self-image and confidence, affecting the way you feel on the inside and creating a different external presence for your brand image.

An interesting take on this subject is in a book called *Labyrinth of Desire* by Rosemary Sullivan, who makes the case that our love relationships are like winding pathways to self-discovery. She writes about love, or the "hot thing we fall into," saying that "...[it] has less to do with finding a mate than with finding the true self one craves to be. For the woman in my story," she writes, "the lover is a vicarious route to some essential part of herself that she does not yet fully recognize or understand... He is the heroic territory she longs to occupy."

Imagine that: the very idea of love—the emotions, the feelings, the chemical reactions it evokes inside every cell in our bodies—is all a manufacturing of our own creation, designed to bring us closer to the inner self and personal truth we so desperately covet.

It makes sense to me, at least on a cerebral level. Isn't that why a part of us is attracted to the bad boy or bad girl? Isn't that why we are aroused by others who are so much like ourselves, even when we know that the combination of two people so right would undoubtedly make a wrong and be completely unsustainable?

He began to think that who you are when
you're with somebody may matter more
than whether you love her.

ANNE TYLER

So what should you do if you're already in a relationship but are now realizing that you've been living a lie? The best thing is to catch yourself in the act whenever you feel that you're being less than who you really are. Start by shaping your future, not by changing your past.

Shedding the façade is hard to do. You can choose to manage the process now or wait and deal with it later. If you wait long enough, the choice may be made for you in the form of a mid-life crisis.

When you're living a lie there is almost always fallout. For most people, mid-life crises occur when they realize that time is ticking, and that they have censored parts of themselves for too long. They hit the boiling point. The spillover is immense—they make changes that are proportional to the size of the lie. For some, a sports car does the trick, but others feel they must wipe the slate clean because they can no longer distinguish between the authentic and false parts of their lives.

All of this has to do with the authenticity we discussed in the first section of this book, but it's particularly relevant in relationships, specifically romantic ones. If the authenticity link is missing or weak, it affects the chain. Eventually the façade will split, causing you to do things that may appear out of character or 'off brand'. But the truth is that your entire brand promise may have been a wrong fit from the start.

The solution is to work on managing your relationships, steering all facets of your being into internal and external alignment. The authenticity gap between your inner and outer self can be bridged with proactive self-discovery, without having to go through the pain and heartache of a crisis. Choose to accept yourself—and your partner—for the amazing individuals you are, whether you remain together or not. And don't try to change him or her into something or someone they're not. It's not fair… to either one of you.

MENTORS

From my first figure skating lesson at age five, through to the time I was twelve, I was blessed to train under the master tutelage of a true saint on skates, Pat Goodridge (now McIntosh). A skilled coach and mentor, she is one of God's disciples here on earth. Being a student of hers came with an unspoken code of conduct and a level of expectation. She led by example; her personal benchmark for success was, and still is, among the highest of anyone I've ever met.

As if by osmosis, her students took on that benchmark and in doing so, they were forever changed as skaters, and as human beings.

We often intuitively know when we are in the presence of greatness. Perhaps it's because, as a wise man once said, "those who bring sunshine to the lives of others cannot keep it from themselves."

The importance of surrounding yourself with mentors can't be stressed enough. Mentors are living, breathing examples of what you would like to do or attain. They may have a personal characteristic you'd like to cultivate, or perhaps they work in a field that interests you. Maybe it's just an emotion you experienced when you first met them — a gut feeling — telling you to learn more about them, and from them. By all means, listen to that inner notion and the little voice inside your head prompting you to find out more. Follow up. Spend time in the company of a true leader... some of it's bound to rub off on you!

> *Great people are those who make others*
> *feel that they, too, can become great.*
>
> MARK TWAIN

In the pursuit and courting of mentors, you'll need persistence (or at least I've needed it). But if I feel strongly enough about someone's potential impact on my life, I stick with it. When I read the book *The Power of Focus* by Jack Canfield, Mark Victor Hansen and Les Hewitt, at the end I glanced at a promotional piece on Achievers Canada (the latter author's company) and discovered that the mailing address was in the same city I had just moved to. That morning I sat down and wrote this email:

—Original Message—
From: Krista Clive-Smith
To: Les Hewitt
Subject: Meeting of the Minds

Hi Les! My name is Krista Clive-Smith. I'm a new resident here in our city, and I am looking to expand my network of successful individuals. Long before I read the book *The Power of Focus,* it had been my policy to invite a new person to lunch each month, and I know that you agree with me on the validity and success that can be gained from just one hour across the table from a brilliant mind! That being said, I'd like to invite you to spend one hour in my company at the restaurant of your choice as my guest sometime during the month of March.
  Please feel free to check out my company website at www.kristaclivesmith.com and to do any other research you feel is necessary prior to accepting my offer, but I encourage you to please seriously consider it nonetheless!

Warm regards,
Krista Clive-Smith

Crazy? Some would say yes, but I'd say I'd have been crazy *not* to write that email. He gave me a half-hour of his time, and during the course of that meeting, the future of the very book you're holding was changed dramatically. I asked a lot of questions, and he was up front and honest, providing me with invaluable advice on the publishing industry through his answers. Then, he started asking me some very tough questions about my direction, about my theories, and about my book.

Learning is acquired by reading books, but the much more necessary learning, the knowledge of the world, is only to be acquired by reading men, and studying all the various editions of them.

LORD CHESTERFIELD

He likely has no idea how much he tested my beliefs about my own abilities that day. But I'm grateful for it. I needed someone to ask those hard questions, to make sure I had answers and had my bases covered. At the end of the conversation, once I had shown that I was serious and totally committed to this project, he opened up his contacts and handed me a pen. Not only did he give me the names and phone numbers of the people who have gone on to become the key members of my production team, but he went the extra mile after I'd left his office and called them to pass along my contact information. I learned more in that half-hour than I've learned in certain years in my lifetime, and I can't imagine what the outcome of this book might have been without the expert collaboration of the editing and layout/design team he recommended. I'm truly grateful for his guidance, direction and inspiration.

A mentor is different from a role model. Mentoring is a two-way street: the information is shared and the ideas are exchanged both ways. In addition to soaking up the information and experiences your mentor describes, it's important to share your own thoughts and philosophies. As a mentor to others, I've often come away learning new things and gaining much from the experience— beyond my feelings of contribution.

When looking for a mentor, think big. Don't assume that you're too small a fish for Mr. or Ms. Famous to talk to. You're not. Be persistent, and be willing to be patient. If the universe deems that you're meant to learn something from your chosen mentor, eventually you will. If not, the lesson might be that you need to hone your ideas about who you're looking for in a mentor!

Treat people as if they were what they ought
to be and help them become what
they are capable of being.

JOHANN WOLFGANG VON GOETHE

Idea Book Exercise

— Guilty By Association—

Write down the names of three couples you admire. What do their relationships have in common? What lessons can you draw upon to make your own partnership more solid?

Relationships   DATE: _____

1. ....

2. ....

3. ....

....

Comments: ....

....

....

....

....

....

The people I view as successful are: ....

....

....

....

....

....

Five relationships I would like to improve over the next six months are:

1.

2.

3.

4.

5.

Comments:

Three wise people I would like to get to know through books are:

1.

2.

3.

YOUR ADVISORY DREAM TEAM:

Choose a personal brand advisory team comprised of five individuals you admire. They can be alive, or from history— real people, or even fictional characters! The responsibility of the Dream Team is to keep you accountable, and balance your brand's strengths and weaknesses. Beside each person's name, explain why you chose him or her and what strengths they bring to the group:

1.

2.

3.

4.

5.

CONCLUSION

I always wanted to be somebody.
Now I realize I should have
been more specific.

LILY TOMLIN (THE 'BAG LADY')

You've developed your personal brand and now you're showing it to the world. You've defined it, positioned it, packaged it and championed it. Now it's up to you to live it. Daily.

The image you've created is a reflection of your authentic self, and you've incorporated both your strengths and your weaknesses into it. If you've completed the exercises and given them a chance to work their magic, you should now be feeling as though your outer and inner selves are well aligned.

Your long-term role as Brand Manager is to repeatedly perform checks to ensure that the three elements — clarity, consistency and authenticity — are present in your brand's image at all times. This will maintain the long term quality control standards and the integrity of your brand.

There'll be times when your inner critic will rear its ugly head and test your confidence. If you're self-employed, for example, you may at times question the rates you're charging, because pricing is often tied directly to your self-esteem when you're a one-person business. If such doubts enter your mind, or when you're feeling insecure, this will be the one and only instance when you should fake it 'til you make it. The only time putting up a façade is a viable proposition is when you're projecting your confidence level to your inner critic. If you need to have a manufactured faith in yourself that you are indeed capable of anything you set your mind to, that's OK. You'll gradually begin to live your way into truly believing that you can. One day you'll wake up and you'll be different: you'll know that you've arrived.

On most highlight reels in sports, there's a clip of the crucial moment in a big game often called the turning point. When you have that awakening - the realization that something's different - you'll have experienced your very own turning point. Mine came on August 18th, sometime between the morning and early afternoon. It appeared to be just like any other Sunday; I'd had a relaxing weekend at the beach with some dear friends, and I was returning to the city by motorcoach. I was writing my six month focus in my Idea Book when the driver's voice came over the intercom and said, "I've just realized that we're on the wrong road. We're going to have to turn the bus around, folks."

The dual significance of those words is haunting. I'd been brainstorming ideas for a second company, and had only just begun to write the six month action plan to launch this new venture when the driver turned the bus around. I'd realized that I, too, was on the wrong road. What I was writing in my Idea Book at that very moment was the metaphorical equivalent to turning my whole life around. But I didn't realize it at the time. I knew that something was different when I woke up the next morning, but it took me years to be able to articulate the events surrounding it and to pinpoint when it actually occurred.

You might wonder, then, how I knew it all happened in an instant, rather than a progressive change over the course of a few days, a week, or even a one-month period. I know because the years... the decades... of body-image issues, self-consciousness, lack of energy and depression that had plagued me had vanished quite literally overnight. They were gone, and they haven't returned to this day. I finally understood — on a very personal level — what it meant to be aligned emotionally, mentally, spiritually, and physically.

It was as though I'd been holding the last piece of the puzzle of who I am for a long, long time. Finally, that day, I turned it a 1/4 turn, and magically, it fit. Then... the puzzle changed from a jigsaw to 3D. But — at that moment, right when it changed — I experienced clarity of vision and a sense of purpose I'd never felt in all my life. And that clarity and purpose has stayed with me every moment since.

> *It is only when we forget all our*
> *learning that we begin to know.*
>
> HENRY DAVID THOREAU

The 3D puzzle that replaced the jigsaw is one that I believe will take an entire lifetime to realize. Bit by bit, day by day, it's a goal to work towards — another step closer to the pinnacle of Maslow's hierarchy of needs.

And as a wise individual once said, "a great life is nothing more than a series of great, well-lived days strung together like a beautiful necklace of pearls."

I can't promise you that it's going to be easy. There are times when you'll feel as though you can't tread another step. There will be voices, whether in the form of the inner critic or in the people that surround you, telling you which parts of your life are best left in the scrap heap. If you allow these voices to be heard, you'll gradually become a mere remnant of the beautiful fabric of what you could be, losing sight of the magic of your own individualism.

You must plan for the worst, hope for the best, and accept what happens. Stay focused on your vision, allowing it to act as your North Star. It'll provide direction, and keep you on the right path—leading you closer to the life you want to live.

Opportunities are never lost; someone will always take the ones you miss. What will fill your heart with the greatest regret at the end of your life will not be all the risks you took—it'll be all those risks you *didn't* take. It may be risky out on a limb, but remember: that's where all the fruit is.

At any given moment you are different—the way you look and feel, and the way you think. And the nature of being human is that you must BE. You must experience. You must share in the glorious triumph of victory and the utter despair of defeat.

Strive to be all you can be. Enjoy being all that you are. It may be for this very moment you exist, so stand up and make a difference. Get noticed. Be remembered. And through it all, just:

Be yourself.

It's a very tough act to follow.

APPENDIX

PERSONAL BRAND CHECKLIST

First Impressions

- ☐ Handshake
- ☐ Personal Introduction/Elevator Speech
- ☐ Eye Contact
- ☐ Body Language
- ☐ Facial Expression(s)
- ☐ Voice
- ☐ Social Media Profile(s) & Posts
- ☐ Business Cards
- ☐ Resume
- ☐ Self Image/Body

Hairstyle

- ☐ Cut
- ☐ Color
- ☐ Style
- ☐ Products

Physical Appearance

- ☐ Teeth/Smile
- ☐ Facial Hair
- ☐ Piercings and Tattoos
- ☐ Makeup
- ☐ Nails/Nail Polish
- ☐ Perfume/Cologne

Accessories

- ☐ Jewelry
- ☐ Eyeglasses
- ☐ Sunglasses
- ☐ Handbag, Wallet and/or Briefcase
- ☐ Hat(s)
- ☐ Business Card Holder
- ☐ Keychain
- ☐ Calendar/Daytimer
- ☐ Cell Phone/Smartphone
- ☐ Pen

Clothing & Shoes

- ☐ Style
- ☐ Color/Patterns
- ☐ Appropriateness
- ☐ Tailoring/Fit
- ☐ Care and Upkeep

Transportation

- ☐ Type of Vehicle (Minivan vs. sports car)
- ☐ Cleanliness, Upkeep, Repair & Maintenance
- ☐ Vehicle Accessories
- ☐ Inside the Trunk of your Car

Your Home

- [ ] Location
- [ ] Décor
- [ ] Setup and/or Layout
- [ ] Possessions
- [ ] The Sensory Experience
- [ ] Your Personal Haven

Your Office

- [ ] Chair(s)
- [ ] Accent Pieces (Area Rugs, Clocks, Lamps, Plants)
- [ ] Artwork/Photos/Wall hangings
- [ ] Desk Accessories
- [ ] Personal Items
- [ ] Souvenirs and/or Collectibles
- [ ] Diplomas, Certificates, Trophies and/or Awards

Brand Champions

- [ ] Your Internal and External Customers (Clients, Bosses, Employees and Co-workers)
- [ ] Your Personal Network: Friends and Acquaintances
- [ ] Family Members
- [ ] Who you Choose to Share your Life with: your Spouse/Partner/Relationship
- [ ] Mentors
- [ ] Your Brand Advisors (Dream Team)
- [ ] Brand Evangelists

ABOUT THE AUTHOR

Krista Clive-Smith (formerly Krista Green) is a recognized expert in the fields of Branding, Organizing, and Business-- the marriage of which creates simplicity and systems... with style. She is seen regularly on the platform speaking at conferences and corporate events, as well as providing training and management consulting for business owners and high performance brands in the U.S. and Canada.

Named to the Top 40 Under 40 list of outstanding young business professionals, she's the author of the book "Get Noticed. Be Remembered." and the 4-Disc Audio Series "How to Brand, Sell, Market and Grow Your Business."

Her first company, Organized for Life, went on to become the first Professional Organizing franchise system worldwide - and the first employer in the industry. Now a real estate investor and serial entrepreneur, Krista currently owns five companies including her newest venture Clutch Branding (a personal brand agency for thought leaders and entrepreneurs with content).

Born and raised in Kamloops, British Columbia, Canada, Krista now makes her home in San Diego, California with the love of her life - her husband Ryan, their daughter Kennedy, her stepdaughter Lindsay, and their dog Cali.

Made in the USA
Monee, IL
05 March 2023

29229872R00125